THE WRITER'S
BOOK OF
WISDOM

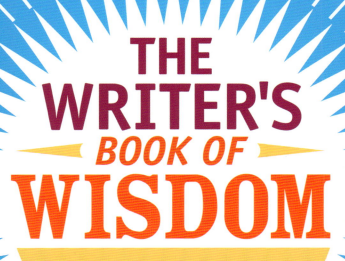

101 RULES
FOR MASTERING
YOUR CRAFT

WRITER'S DIGEST BOOKS
CINCINNATI, OHIO
www.writersdigest.com

STEVEN TAYLOR GOLDSBERRY

The Writer's Book of Wisdom. © 2005 by Steven Taylor Goldsberry. Manufactured in China. All rights reserved. No part of this book may be reproduced in any form or by any electronic or mechanical means including information storage and retrieval systems without permission in writing from the publisher, except by a reviewer, who may quote brief passages in a review. Published by Writer's Digest Books, an imprint of F+W Publications, Inc., 4700 East Galbraith Road, Cincinnati, OH 45236. (800) 289-0963. First edition.

Visit our Web site at www.writersdigest.com for information on more resources for writers.

To receive a free weekly e-mail newsletter delivering tips and updates about writing and about Writer's Digest products, register directly at our Web site at http://newsletters.fwpublications.com.

09 08 07 06 05   5 4 3 2 1

Library of Congress Cataloging-in-Publication Data

Goldsberry, Steven.
　The writer's book of wisdom: 101 rules for mastering your craft / by Steven Taylor Goldsberry.
　　p. cm.
　ISBN 1-58297-292-3 (alk. paper)
　　1. Authorship. I. Title.
PN147.G595 2004　　　　　　　　　　2004053033
808'.02—dc22　　　　　　　　　　　　CIP

Edited by Kelly Nickell
Designed by Lisa Buchanan
Cover by Lisa Buchanan
Page layout by Matthew DeRhodes
Production coordinated by Robin Richie
Interior illustrations © CSA Images

NOTE TO READERS

Readers sensitive to this sort of thing may take issue with the author's use of "he" and "him" as singular pronouns identifying any general person, rather than "she," "her," "he/she," "him/her," "he or she," "him or her," or the increasingly accepted "understood as singular" usage of "they" and "them."

This is a stylistic choice, motivated by literary convention and a desire for speed in communication, and implies no gender inequities. You may substitute any of the above pronoun options where appropriate.

ABOUT THE AUTHOR

Steven Taylor Goldsberry (M.F.A., Ph.D., Iowa) is professor of English at the University of Hawai'i, a Michener Fellow, and instructor at the Maui Writers Retreat. He has been teaching creative writing and composition for twenty-five years. His books include *Maui the Demigod, Luzon, Over Hawai'i, Sunday in Hawai'i,* and *The First 16 Secrets of Chi*.

ACKNOWLEDGMENTS

Many thanks to the following people, some of them students, but all teachers as well: Robert Morris, John Tullius, Shannon Tullius, John Saul, Michael Sack, Bryce Courtenay, Andy Cohen, Terry Brooks, Judine Brooks, Elizabeth George, Don McQuinn, Carol McQuinn, Joe Ortiz, Katherine Ramsland, Dan Millman, David Fryxell, Melanie Rigney, Chris Vogler, Alice Plato, Dorothy Allison, Rita Rosencranz, Jewelle Gomez, Sam Horn, Jay Leite, Craig Lesley, Raymond Obstfeld, Pat Quinn, Richard Santos, Barbara Santos, Kate Ryan, Georja Skinner, Diana Wentworth, Roger Jellinek, Eden-Lee Murray, Liz Cratty, Al Cratty, Deborah Iida, Bob Mayer, Paula Danziger, Tad Bartimus, Jack Canfield, Patrick von Weigant, Robin Gainey, Rachel Funk, Billy Letts, Nancy Holder, Susan Wiggs, Robert Giffin, Joe Marich, Linda Michaels, Marilyn Wooley, Kam Napier, Jonathan Padua, Tom Paxton, Robert Prete, Veronica Randall, Sara Rice, Will Schwalbe, Jeff Schwartz, Mauka, Jay Bonansinga, Jeannie Bonansinga, Nancy Carraway, Neil Abercrombie, Greg Poirier, Elizabeth Stead, Eric Paul Shaffer, Steve Weingartner, Gay Wong, Bennett Hymer, Rita Ariyoshi, Jessica Yerega, Wanda Adams, Burl Burlingame, Paul Atkins, Gracie Atkins, Robert Barclay, Nolan Kim, Bill Danks, Gavan Daws, Dave Porter, Ozzie Bushnell, Betty Bushnell, William Foltz, Angie Flaherty, Brandon Sutherlin, Eddie Sherman, Diane Rubio, Cheryl Irebaria, Jeff Wallace, Claudia Wallace, Garrett Hatakenaka, Lucy Finnigan, Paula Polk, Perry N. Daniel, Michael Manning, Lora Cawelti, Krystalynn Ontai, Ian Macmillan, Robert Onopa, Gay Sibley, Robbie Shappard, Marc Myer, Earl Nawatani, Jeanine Denis, E.L. Doctorow, Julia Groh, Jeffry Lapin, Kim Taylor Reece, Kanoe Reece, Yvonne Chotzen, Stuart Coleman, C. Mark Hood, Dick Katz, Vance Bourjaily, Stanley Plumly, Marvin Bell, Donald Justice, Robert Stone, Jack Unterecker, Phyllis Hoge Thompson, Phil Damon, Frank Stewart, Steve Curry, Morgan Blair, Nell Altizer, William Dickey, John Logan, Maxine Hong Kingston, Richard Paul Evans, Sheryl Fullerton, Jane Hopkins, Eric Landstrom, Dietrich Varez, Herb Kane, Robert Tippets, Gordon Thomas, Sidney Jenson, Jay Fox, Ned Williams.

Special thanks to my brilliant and patient editor, Kelly Nickell, to my agent, Laurie Liss, to my colleagues in the English department at the University of Hawai'i, and to all of the faculty and staff at the Maui Writers Conference and Retreat.

And to Ui most of all, as always. To Micah, and Haunani and Pancho, and to the extended family Goldsberry, Spurrier, James, Manning, Sullivan, Schmeling, Aadnesen, Taylor, Johnson, Dickerson, and Kanekoa.

TABLE OF CONTENTS

PART 2: LANGUAGE

INTRODUCTION

These are the elements of writing, and they have nothing to do with style. The basics of prose are simple and universal. I never teach style, I teach these elements.
—Bryce Courtenay

It begins early with a piece of writing. A clever title flags us down, and then the author entrances us with a dazzling opening page. Pretty soon we're off, traveling in a dream world created for our enjoyment and edification. We've discovered something new, and we have to find out what happens next because it's suddenly important to us.

No matter what kind of writing you produce—poetry, fiction, nonfiction, plays, essays, or reports—there are widely accepted conditions that must be met or readers will probably look elsewhere.

Besides being engaging, the work has to get better with each sentence, and lead inalterably to a climax, a big payoff for our time. The longer the work, the more electrifying the climax.

But do keep all of your creations as brief as possible. Speed in communication is the key, using just the right words in just the right amount.

How you shape those words and exhibit them in a professional manner is what this book is about. *The Writer's Book of Wisdom* derives its authority from the art of storytelling, which, for the last three centuries, has been practiced most effectively by novelists and short story writers. The assumptions here are twofold: first, that if you've mastered the skills needed to write a novel, you can write anything; and, second, that no matter what the genre, all writing is storytelling.

Therefore, the best way to learn your craft is to study what fiction writers do. Analyze their workmanship—the descriptive gems in character sketches and setting, story lines shaped by well-paced narrative, poetry in lyrical passages, philosophical statements, scenes with people talking to each other—in short, life rendered in humanity's most eclectic art form. A practicing writer versed in storytelling techniques has limitless potential. So let's get these fundamentals down.

The 101 rules presented here have expanded from hundreds of attempts over the years, by my students and me, to write the best advice possible for writers. Most of these brief rules include tips for editing your own work and some suggestions for further reading. The book ends with the handy "Evaluation Guide for Writing," a checklist of questions to ask about your manuscript drafts.

You can read the rules straight through, or skip around. Peruse the Table of Contents and look up whatever sounds most interesting.

The Writer's Book of Wisdom is designed for beginners, but as every seasoned writer knows, we're all beginners, perpetual rookies no matter our age or accomplishment. And the more we learn and practice, the more we realize our vast ignorance.

AN ASSIGNMENT

Thoreau says in *Walden* that when people talk, they should be in a large room with enough distance between them so their long sentences have a chance to unfold properly from mouth to ear. The written voice needs distance too, and more of it. Isolation is what suits our craft. Besides, for most of us insecure beings the old definition applies: A man of letters is someone who stays home and tries through his writing to impress the world, because he knows his going out in public won't do it.

Writers prefer this arrangement. We are, in fact, like Hobbits, about whom Tolkien said, "Their elusiveness is due solely to a professional skill." We perform better that way. Our greatest work for humans is accomplished as far from humans as we can get.

Now, before you read another word about how to write, go off by yourself where you can practice at least the mechanical beauty of putting words into print—where your sentences can unfold. Journey, good artist, to the remote habitat of your desk, spread out a sheet of paper as wide and quiet as an open field ...

And begin.

> *Good friends who come to read this book,*
> *Strip yourselves first of affectation.*
> —François Rabelais, *Gargantua and Pantagruel*

PART 1

APPROACH

#1

RULE # 1

LEARN THE RULES BEFORE YOU BREAK THEM

Rule \ 'rül \ n. Wisdom based upon experience, articulated.

There are no absolute "rules" for good writing, only guidelines that have proven successful. Those who break the rules are the true artists. However, learn, practice, and master the rules first.

Notice the circular logic of that first paragraph. It seems profound and liberating, but then it cracks a surreptitious whip.

Read it again.

What it says is rules aren't important, but they are.

It says rules are artificial structures; great art is a lofty enterprise that soars above such limitations; but in order to fly you need a structure from which to launch.

In elementary and secondary education today there are some English teachers telling their students, "Write anything you want. Don't worry about spelling, grammar, or organization. Just write down whatever pops into your head."

Fear and ignorance perpetuate this error in pedagogy: fear that a critical approach might discourage self-esteem; and ignorance of the reason behind the rules. The only place for free writing of this sort—and it should be absolutely encouraged here—is the first draft, the one that won't be handed in for a grade. Brainstorming has to be uninhibited. After that, students should fix their work to make it better.

And speedier.

So, herein lies the purpose for all the rules: If the artist fails to follow them, the audience becomes distracted. Rules exist for the sake of efficiency. If your reader has to struggle to understand what you mean, he does so at the expense of your story.

Bad craft gets in the way. It's like listening to a storyteller who has the wretched habit of clicking his teeth. Or repeating the phrase, "You know." He means well, and he has a first-rate drama to entertain you with, but here come those clicks and repetitions.

In his slovenly presentation he has ignored propriety, lost control of his medium, and created something more than a pure tale. And that more, in this case, diminishes the story. You know. Click. More is less.

For the sake of clarity, for success, follow the rules. And then, when you've become a veteran craftsman, break them so subtly it's almost impossible to notice.

Trust the judgment of your readers. If it seems to them you've made a mistake rather than broken the rules for effect, you've made a mistake.

> *You cannot transcend what you do not know.*
> —Sri Nisargadatta Maharaj

WRITING IS MORE CRAFT THAN ART

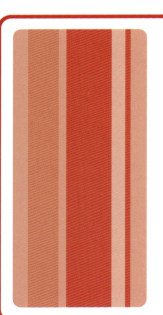

Anyone can learn it with discipline and practice.

Writers write. More importantly, they write along a learning curve and improve with each word. It's like sports. The more you exercise the stronger you get. Unlike sports, where the body eventually gives out, your mind will keep you in the writing game.

Study the craft by doing it. Write. Everyday.

BELIEVE IN YOURSELF EVEN IF NO ONE ELSE DOES

Michael Crichton enrolled at Harvard with the intention of becoming a writer, but he got Cs on his English papers. He was eighteen and, he admitted, "vain about my writing and I felt it was Harvard, and not I, that was in error. So I decided to make an experiment." He boldly plagiarized an essay by George Orwell and handed it in as his own. If caught, he would be expelled. But he figured that any professor who would give him a C probably hadn't read enough great literature to notice. Orwell's writing received a B-. And that convinced Crichton that "the English department was too difficult." So he switched majors and probably delayed by several years the beginning of his writing career.

While Crichton proved his point, he made a cardinal mistake.

If you think you're supposed to be a writer, if you have a passion for it, if you read books thinking, "I can do this," if you stay up sleepless in the quiet of the night because you have to put your thoughts on paper, if you cross them out and write them again until they sound right, if you have things to say that could make life better for someone (especially you, your first and most critical reader), then don't let to any damned bloated and pedigreed authority figure tell you otherwise.

You're a writer.

It takes a hell of a lot of work to be a good one. Don't kid yourself. Lots of sleepless nights. Years of study (look at how long it took Crichton). But hardship never stopped you before. You've proven yourself elsewhere and can do so again.

And what is writing, after all? A craft. Like knitting. Woodworking. Forging swords. It just takes more practice, and a fiercely self-generated conviction in your own ability.

By the way, Michael Crichton has, to date, earned more money than any author in history.

It is requisite for the ideal artist to possess a force of character that seems hardly compatible with its delicacy; he must keep his faith in himself while the incredulous world assails him with its utter disbelief; he must stand up against mankind and be his own sole disciple ...
—Nathaniel Hawthorne, "The Artist of the Beautiful"

#4

4

TRUE INSPIRATION MUST BE EARNED
BY WRITING

If you wait to be inspired before you start writing, if you wait to experience that bolt of soul-clarifying insight, you're a fool and have no business being a writer.

Write. The physical act itself will free the imagination.

In this sense writing is like dancing, or sports, where the expression of grace comes only through movement.

There's a stylistic technique in literary fiction known as stream of consciousness, and that should be the strategy of your first draft. Whatever words flow into your brain, let them continue to flow through your fingertips.

At least in its initial phase, writing is easy. One word after another. Inspiration usually comes mid-sentence. Your muse will sing, but only to the accompaniment of coursing ink.

Inspiration? A hoax that poets have invented to give themselves importance.
—Jean Anouilh

#5

5

WRITE TO BE GREAT, NOT RICH

If you're getting into writing to make money, get back out.

As a career, writing attracts more people than any other field in the arts. Average pay for writers has dropped 30 percent in the last twenty years. It's a crowded profession, and only those who love it regardless of financial reward can sustain themselves for very long. Money may be realized, but as a consequence and not a goal.

Robert Frost said that to be truly happy is to wed your vocation to your avocation, to figure out how to make a pastime pay.

Much of it has to do with drive, with seeing a project through to the end. Professional writers complete a book and then work hard to get it published.

It's true that some people have advantages in the market. Beyond their actual writing (or ghosted help), they might claim friends or relatives in the business. Maybe a stellar or notorious career has already put them in the limelight, and they trade on that.

Pure luck can give someone an edge.

Maybe you have none of that. Maybe all you have is the truth of your writing. But the stories you must tell, and the rigorous training you pursue, will coalesce into certain power.

Keep in mind the words of author William Faulkner in his 1950 Nobel acceptance speech. He said that the writer, through "anguish and travail," endeavors "to create out of the materials of the human spirit something which did not exist before," and that the only subject matter worthy of such labor is "the problems of the human heart in conflict with itself."

Nobility of purpose will see you through.

Train one eye on the mountain peak, the other on the path. Enjoy the climb. The journey is its own reward.

In my drive to write, there was a dream of glory, of being a first-rate writer. I didn't want money and fame. I only wanted to say what I thought was important. If I had not set my sights on being great, I would not even have been good today. No one promised me anything. There was never any assurance of my talent nor that anyone would read one line that I would write.
There was nothing that I could have for the asking. I had to earn it. Most of all, I never wrote for the money. Writing is not a business. Writing is an art.
—Katherine Anne Porter

GET USED TO
DESPAIR

And keep on writing, of course.

You will have critics bent on keeping you down, none more ruthless than your own mad, cruel self. Your friends, who long ago judged you as superior and aloof, will experience a secret apoplexy when you announce you're a writer. They will say, "Good for you. Get that book published." But their hearts will darken with envy and an unwavering belief in your incompetence. After you succeed, they'll say, "What are you working on now?" Thinking, *He can't do it again.* The more you do it, the more they'll accept that you are what you said you are. And then you'll attract critics and reviewers, many of whom are professionals at envy. Not only will they be certain of your incompetence, they will analyze and broadcast it.

Of all the arts, writing is perhaps the most difficult. It's not a performing art, so you don't have the immediacy of a live audience to let you know how you're doing. It's only black marks on white paper, so it's not pretty like painting or architecture. Everyone thinks he can do it, so it has little prestige. It can be lonely work.

Little wonder, then, that in the film *The Owl and the Pussycat*, George Segal's character, a writer in New York, takes his portable typewriter to Central Park, chucks it over a hill and says, "That damned thing almost killed me."

Are you sure you want to be a writer?

If so, you must be willing to embrace the inevitable despair that accompanies meaningful creation.

No matter how piercing and appalling his insights, the desolation creeping over his outer world, the lurid lights and shadows of his inner world, the writer must live with hope, work in faith.
—J.B. Priestley

FAIL

Fail well.

Fail with training.

Take a shot. You may miss. But failure is a better teacher than success. Think of the shot itself as a victory.

Go to the blackboard and write your contribution to the class. The teacher may not like it. Or she might. Either way, you will return to the board tomorrow. Your purpose is to please, and please again.

That old maxim "failure is not an option" never applies to art. Think of it like surfing, where falling down is the first thing you have to learn. The only real failure comes by not trying to stand at all.

Fail without fear.

You always pass failure on the way to success.
—Mickey Rooney

KEEP YOUR WRITING EXERCISES IN
PERSPECTIVE

If you want someone else to tell you what to write, there are lots of starred books and degree-holding instructors out there brimming with assignments.

Most people appreciate direction. Go ahead, buy the books. Attend the classes. Write what you're told to write. If you need that. Hack writers crave structure. Be a hack for a while. It's good training.

If you find a writing exercise to be confining or bland, do it anyway. Imagine using the text as part of a future book. Save all your manuscripts. Stephen King's *Hearts in Atlantis* combines new text with an old novella he wrote just out of college. After his first big score, John Grisham pulled out *A Time to Kill*, the first book he had published (only five thousand copies), revised it, and made a new sale. The first John Gardner book to see print was the seventh book he wrote, the second published was the sixth one he wrote, and so on. He had stored away all his projects knowing that after his breakthrough he could recycle them.

Acquiesce to your heart's demands. The Hemingway slogan "write what you know" will pull you beyond relying on outside motivation. Ultimately, you know better than your teachers.

You may be one of those exceptional, autodidactic writers who needs no instruction at all. But be aware of the first two questions a professional editor may ask when you approach him with your manuscript: "What is the title of your book?" (The answer will indicate the originality of your style.) And, "Have you had any formal training?" (Which will show that you've paid your dues in writing workshops.)

A naïve attitude might even help. A lot of people have accomplished great things simply because they didn't know they couldn't. Edward Gibbon, who authored the gargantuan *Rise and Fall of the Roman Empire*, made this alarming statement:

> *Unproved with original learning, unformed in the habits of thinking, unskilled in the arts of composition, I resolved to write a book.*

#9

RULE # 9

BE PREPARED TO FIGHT YOUR DEMONS

Writing is seduction. Writing is war. Writing is scary and sublime. Even if you don't get published, writing will help you figure out almost everything: subject, emotion, and spirit.

We scribblers can't help ourselves. Whatever comes into our heads we put on paper. The good and the bad. We report first to ourselves, and then to anyone who will listen.

In the process of telling the truth, we become better, but not without facing the pain of that truth.

Be strong and face it.

Writing works as therapy, for you and for your readers.

#10

RULE # 10

STAY OUT
OF SIGHT

Ego can kill art. Obviously you need some ego to presume to create. But this isn't about you. It's about something greater. You are merely a conduit.

Whatever it is you wish to bring to the page, you are its servant, its coachman, its loyal and unobtrusive scribe.

"Children should be seen but not heard," the old saying goes. Writers should be heard but not seen.

Writers, who tend to be shy, get to stay home and still be public.
—Anne Lamott, *Bird by Bird*

#11

11

WORK IN
AN INSPIRING
ENVIRONMENT

Whatever you need to set the mood for serious creativity, go ahead and spoil yourself. Beyond flashes of inspiration or hurried note-taking, beyond composition under duress when you've got a deadline to meet, there will be moments when the best thoughts come to you.

Play classical music, perhaps light a single symbolic candle, and read your favorite literature during these sessions.

Some writers prefer the silence of late night or early morning, when the neighborhood sleeps. Others seek enlightenment at dawn. Stephen King claims to write in the morning while listening to hard rock, and he says that all writing is telepathy, meaning that it's beamed from some noncorporeal brain into his own. (How it gets through Guns and Roses only King knows.) Most artists call this telepathic phenomenon the imagination, and it works best by itself, without too many external distractions.

That single candle you light may be a desk lamp or the glow of your computer screen. Let it provide a pool of light that shines only upon your manuscript. And it will surely illuminate—eventually, at least after many long hours of rewrites—genius.

#12

12

THINK OF WRITING SESSIONS AS ENTERTAINMENT

Better than going to the stadium to root for the home team, certainly better than attending a community theater production (almost always performed by amateurs), better than concerts, television, movies.

Your thoughts and words are easily as interesting to explore as any prepackaged commercial confection. To write a story or an essay is to watch its drama unfold.

If writing isn't fun for you, how can you expect anyone to have fun reading your work?

Your "hot ticket" seat is next to no one, in a crowd of one, at the desk. Honor the first duty of the writer, which is to entertain readers, and entertain your steadfast first reader: yourself.

#13

ELECTRONIC VOICES DESTROY INSPIRATION

Television is a rectangular drain. Turn it on and you pull the plug on creativity. Sure, there are shows like *The West Wing* that will inspire you. And movies on DVD to learn from. Take time away and watch those. Then turn off the box and open your work-in-progress. Radio is the same. Don't have it on while you're writing, especially "talk radio." With all those other voices filling the air, how can you hear your muse?

Listen to books on tape when you're driving or when you get stuck during a writing session. Let those words inspire you to achieve your own goals.

Inspiration moves in waves like a radio signal, but at such a high frequency you can pick it up only when the band is clear of outside chatter. Remember what Groucho Marx once so famously declared:

> *I find television very educating. Every time somebody turns on the set, I go into the other room and read a book.*

You should go *write* a book.

#14

RETURN TO
THE BASICS

Some of the time, at least, you should revert to the old way, that smooth and silent transfer of thought directly onto the page. Compose with pen and paper.

Legend has it that the Marquis de Sade, imprisoned in the Charenton asylum where they deprived him of ink and quills, wrote on the walls using his own blood and the point of a fingernail.

The impulse to dirty our hands must hearken back to the dawn of man, when Paleolithic artists crushed charcoal into water and applied it to the surface of flat rock. We have an ancestral, even spiritual, desire to create by hand.

A keyboard will never give you that same satisfaction. Keyboards are publishing tools. Look at the word manuscript. The Latin translation says it all: *manu* means *by hand*; *scriptus* means *written*.

Return to your roots once in a while.

GENERATE
TEXT

Freewriting, the act of recording whatever comes into your head for a given period of time, costs nothing, except a little ink and time. It takes no preparation, no scheduling, no plan. Certainly no inspiration.

The goal is to get something down. On paper. It will be full of junk, of course, "mucho crappo," as playwright Miguel Piñero calls it, but that doesn't matter. No one will see it but you.

You may have heard this story before, but it's so good it bears repeating.

Sinclair Lewis, who was America's first Nobel laureate in literature, received an invitation from Harvard to lecture about writing. He showed up drunk.

When he took the stage, he yelled at the students, "Hands up, all those who want to be writers!"

Of course, everyone held up a hand.

"Then why the hell aren't you home writing?" he asked, and staggered away. End of lecture.

Whether you're a beginner or seasoned professional, the process is the same. Get started with one word and add to it. Stay seated until you complete a draft. Australian novelist Bryce Courtenay says, the secret to success is "bum glue." Sit on your butt and create. Writing is a sedentary activity. And hooray for that. You could do worse things sitting down.

When you must sit, it should only be to play a musical instrument, to watch your children, to look out upon the fashioned expanse of your manual labors, to eat your meals, or to write.
—Baxter S. Marbury

#16

RULE # 16

BREAK AWAY FROM
YOUR LABORS

1
2
3
4
5
6
7
8
9
10
11
12
13
14
15
16
17
18
19
20
21
22
23
24
25
26
27
28
29
30
31
32
33

You know you're up too late writing when a story about a strange earl in medieval London strikes you. He is a mysterious character, often seen skulking around the streets at midnight. He becomes known as the Midnight Earl. The citizens eventually accuse him of witchcraft and burn him at the stake. You title your story "Burning the Midnight Earl."

This is what's called a red flag moment. Red flag! Red flag! Time to run away!

Sure, you want to be dedicated and relentless about out-working your competition. Do it. But then you have to close the manuscript and pursue something else.

Hemingway said he made a point of exercising a lot in order to stay in top physical shape for those long stints of writing when inspiration really hit.

Inspiration is not hitting if you are burning the Midnight Earl. Understand? Keep your body healthy.

As an artist, you only get better with age. Don't neglect yourself for your work. Stay well.

#17

STOP READING
THIS BOOK

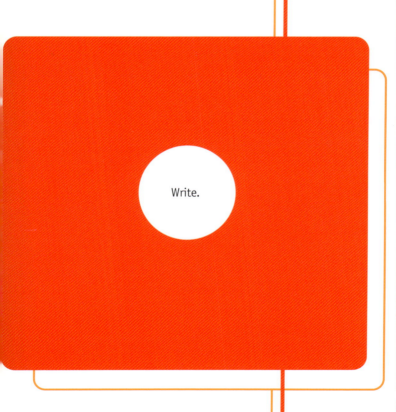

Write.

18

RESIST
DISTRACTIONS

Sometimes the universe conspires to lure you away from your sacred calling.

The difficulty of the craft might hold you back. Don't let it. Just because something's hard, that it taxes your emotions, stamina, imagination, or will, is no reason to quit.

Other things that are easier or more fun will tempt you. Chocolate chip cookies. Shooting hoops. Mowing the lawn. You know, almost *anything* else.

Nonwriters seem so carefree. Think of them as idiots—maybe that will help.

And now here's a strange fact. Your fellow scribblers might be your worst enemies.

Folks with shared interests congregate, talk shop. But writers are pretty relentless about their little cadres and coteries. They attend readings, workshops, conferences. And all of this is fine. A good writers retreat every couple of years can rev you like those friction spinners on your old HotWheels set. But, as Stephen King says, "The hours we spend talking about writing is time we don't spend actually doing it."

This is a book to inspire you to write, not to keep you from it. Read it for a few minutes and return to your keyboard.

Press on: Nothing in the world can take the place of perseverance. Talent will not; nothing is more common than unsuccessful men with talent. Genius will not; unrewarded genius is almost a proverb. Education will not; the world is full of educated derelicts. Persistence and determination alone are omnipotent.

—Calvin Coolidge

There are lots of terrific writers out there, and usually the difference between them and published authors is that the authors finish.

#19

PRODUCE MULTIPLE **DRAFTS**

Anne Lamott refers to the first draft as the down draft and the second as the up draft, because you get it down then fix it up. Stephen King calls the first one the "closed door" draft and the second the "open door," the first being for you alone and the second for others to see.

You should write at least three drafts, however. Author Robert Stone insists on this number, explaining that in the first stage he writes very quickly, recording things as they come off the top of his head. The second draft he approaches more intensely, revising the diction and syntax to give it literary power. And the third draft he uses to make it all sound like it's just coming off the top of his head.

Writers early in their careers will need many more than three; ten is advised.

The longer you work and the more you generate text, the sooner you'll produce a manuscript that someone wants to read.

What is written without effort is read without pleasure.
—Samuel Johnson

#20

RULE # 20

THINK OF YOUR FIRST DRAFT AS A BLUE-BOOK
ESSAY EXAM

You remember the blue books teachers used to pass out for exams? You would crack one open when your instructor said, "Begin," and you wrote as fast as your mind could move the pencil. Your middle finger got a cupped indentation from the wooden shaft where it rested while you wrote hard. Barely thinking. Scribbling until your penmanship went awobble. You erased the indecipherable words, slowed down, and the wrote them again. Fast.

So, when you compose your first draft, just pretend that you're taking an essay exam. You have only until the end of the hour to finish. Your grade depends on it. You really have to finish because an incomplete blue book will make you look stupid.

The point is: Get that whole draft done from start to finish.

Unlike school, you have the luxury at your home desk of being able to polish it once it's done.

But you must finish. Now! The bell's going to ring!

You have only so much time to complete your answer.

21

RULE # 21

IGNORE THE LENGTH OF YOUR
FIRST DRAFT

A piece of writing is organic, like a tree. It grows to maturity, to its adult size, and stops all by itself. So when you're working on your first draft, indulge in its beguiling nuances, in its open space and infinite possibility. Fine. Go with it. Write as much as you want.

Pruning is essential, however. Trees bear more fruit when trimmed. Alexander Pope made nearly the same observation, though much more poetically, in his "Essay on Criticism":

Words are like leaves; and where they most abound,

Much fruit of sense beneath is rarely found.

Cutting away at a full-grown creation that you have nurtured from seed, so to speak, can be tough. You tend to cherish every bit of its magnificence. But you have to get mean and discipline yourself. Most readers want you to be frugal and direct.

Editors are readers too, professional readers, and advocates for the reading public. Anticipate their concerns about space requirements and printing costs. Generally speaking, the shorter the manuscript, the greater the chances of its being published.

PRACTICE
MECHANICAL
LEARNING

Herman Melville's Bartleby was a scrivener. A copier of texts. He made a living—this was before cheap printing and Xerox machines—by reproducing documents by hand with a quill and ink well. One day he decided to passively resist work, telling his employer, "I would prefer not to."

As an exercise, try being a positive Bartleby. This may sound strange, but it's a terrific lesson. Copy the first 1,000 words of your favorite book, word for word. Copy it longhand, then sit at your keyboard and type it up.

Copy slowly, no rush. Make sure to replicate all punctuation as you find it in the original.

What this exercise does is get you on the same spiritual course that your author charted, following the precise physical motions he used to produce the masterpiece.

It won't seem such an odd activity if you think of writing as music. Rather than composing your own symphony, you're playing a master's, each note as he wrote it.

This form of mechanical learning will help you on some elemental level, like inscribing a code for cellular memory.

Consciously, you won't get it. Consciously, it may seem like a stupid waste of time. But after you do it, you'll sense its value by instinct.

One copy is enough, unless you want to continue because you've begun to feel an agreeable magic in the process. Try it as many times as you like, with different writers and genres. Bartleby had to copy legal documents; maybe that's why he quit. You have the choice of the finest literature.

"I want to write like J.K. Rowling," people have said. Write *her* first, instead of *like* her. See what doors open with that wizard's key.

RECOMMENDED READING

The short story "Bartleby the Scrivener" by Herman Melville. Overly long and sometimes as boring as the title character himself, but an unforgettable tale.

#23

SEEK THE WISDOM OF OTHERS

People outside the business often say that writers create in a vacuum. Alone in their own heads. Lost to another world. The source of your vision and first attempts at articulating it are, to be sure, fiercely personal. But when it comes to communicating that vision most effectively, you have to get advice from outside experts.

Critique groups bring you into contact with talented writers. Join one. Share your work, and have others share theirs with you. Unlike criticism offered by friends and family, you'll receive unbiased feedback from fellow craftsmen. Learn from their suggestions and from their mistakes.

Whatever revisions they suggest, let some fall away. Make use of the ones you like; discard the junk. Never argue about or defend your work. Simply listen. Criticism will follow you no matter where you go, so get used to it. And grow from it. You're on your way to being a professional.

#24

RULE #  **24**

KEEP YOURSELF
OPEN TO
SERENDIPITY

According to legend, this is how Styrofoam was invented. A chemist was mixing ingredients in a cup, made a mistake in measurement, and put the mixture over a flame. What bubbled up hardened into a substance he'd never seen before: an airy but solid material that we now see everywhere, in packing material, toys, surfboards, coffee cups.

Say you mistype a word, or mishear what someone said, but it inspires you.

You meant to type pigs, but wrote pits instead. It leads you to compose a children's story about a cast-off peach pit, olive pit, and mango pit becoming friends. *The Three Little Pits*.

You have an odd uncle named Fred, and you accidentally type in a letter, "Dear Unclue Fred." But that seems to fit him better.

You might pick up an odd combination of names. A French couple named Dipité has a daughter Sarah. A Chinese couple named Ho has a daughter Heidi. Comedy ensues.

Serendipity, strange coincidences, can lead to great ideas for your writing. Consider these things as subtle gifts from the muses.

BORROW (AND STEAL) FROM YOUR FAVORITE WRITERS

> *The secret to creativity is knowing how to hide your source.*
> —Albert Einstein

If you read a book long enough, the music of the language drifts into your head in such a way that when you turn to your own writing you'll be humming someone else's tune. In Raymond Carver's fiction you hear the early John Cheever. Hundreds of American writers imitated the Hemingway style. Every French poet in the late nineteenth century tried to sing like Whitman.

Which is fine. Other writers, past and present, are your models, and your competition. You have to read them to beat them, and you do that by using their heads as stepping-stones.

There's plagiarism (bad), and then there's creative plagiarism. With the latter, if you're skillful at it, you won't get caught. "Plagiarize," Tom Lehrer sang, "Let no one else's work evade your eyes. Remember why the good Lord made your eyes." Plagiarize.

You know Shakespeare swiped all of his plots, boldly retelling stories someone else had written. He even filched a phrase here and there. If anyone noticed they hardly cared. His brilliant inventiveness so blinded them to the old that they received a whole new vision.

Only by taking art from a master and reprocessing it as your own will you achieve your destiny. Athletes and musicians do this all the time, replicating movements and riffs they admire, doing them over hundreds of times and embellishing upon the originals.

The quote that teaches the rule best is an old saw, one that's been stolen so many times no one knows who said it first: "Good writers borrow; great writers steal."

How do they get away with it? Great writers are cat burglars. They sneak into the canonical mansion, come away with only a few select jewels, and hide them in their own house. No one's the wiser.

So keep an open book by your favorite writer next to your work-in-progress, for purposes of inspiration and imitation. Have no fear of losing your soul with this practice. No matter how influential someone else's art might be, your personality will remain undiminished. Your clear voice will blend with and be further clarified by others. But you will always be you. In the words of Martha Graham, "There is a vitality, a life force, a quickening that is translated through you into action, and because there is only one of you in all time, this expression is unique."

When you write something as good as what your favorite writer has written, you can sell it. The game is that simple.

Imitation is not just the sincerest form of flattery—it's the sincerest form of learning.
—George Bernard Shaw

#26

26

ALWAYS HAVE A NOTEBOOK AND PEN ON HAND

You know why. You're a writer.

Sometimes you feel like the last rhinoceros in the *Jumanji* stampede. This will help you gain on the rest of your competitors: Work all the time.

#27

27

KEEP A "READ-IN-PROGRESS" NEARBY

If you go anywhere, take a book with a pen wedged between the pages instead of some fancy-dancy bookmark. This is so you can underline, and make notes. Marginalia might lead to manuscripts.

Paperbacks are best for this, obviously. Smaller ones can fit in your pocket.

When you're stuck (fully stopped) in a traffic jam, standing in line, waiting for a bus, sitting through a boring sermon, riding in a car with the family—whenever something less interesting than a book is going on around you—read.

The classics may not be necessary for the happiness of a bond salesman, but they are indispensable for our community of writers. It is from these enduring works that we form a reservoir of insight and allusion.
—James Kilpatrick

CREATE AN ANTHOLOGY OF YOUR FAVORITE **LITERATURE**

Get yourself a scrapbook and fill it with scraps of words.

These are the indispensable texts. Your bible of crafted scripture. Here lie the sentences that inspire you to write.

Find one good sentence and copy it down. Make a page of such sentences. Whole paragraphs even. Copy them. Copy a page's worth of stuff.

Excerpts also work well. Articles from a magazine. Handouts from an English class. Use only writing that you want to keep and enshrine in your personal anthology.

Call it *Stone Soup for the Mind*. Its only organizing principle is that it's a history of ideas.

You've heard of stone soup. It comes from an old European folktale about a wandering man who was as clever as he was poor. He carried with him a pot and an ordinary stone the size of a potato. He had no other belongings except for a ladle, a bowl, and a spoon. In each village he came to, he built a small fire where the villagers could see it. He drew water from a nearby stream, and put his pot to boil above the flames.

People always came to watch this stranger. He would drop the stone into the steaming pot and stir the water. Then, in every village, something like this happened:

"What's that you've got cooking?" a woman asked.

"Stone soup," said the poor traveler. "Would you like a taste?" He raised a ladleful, and blew to cool it. "You will find the flavor unique."

The woman took a sip, held it in her mouth for a while, and swallowed. "Quite unusual," she said, "but I think it needs carrots. May I bring some from my garden?"

"It would please me to add your carrots to my soup," said the man. "And bring a bowl. Join me for supper."

"I will," said the grateful woman.

Another woman asked for a taste, and said, "Onions. It needs my fine onions."

"They would certainly strengthen the brew," said the man.

After these women added the carrots and onions, other villagers took turns trying the soup. Each one offered to add another ingredient, a garlic clove from this one, a turnip from that, a bunch of green beans, a box of potatoes, a chicken, etc.

The villagers all brought their bowls with their offerings of food. They had a grand feast. And everyone agreed upon one thing: The stone soup was the best they had ever tasted.

Make an anthology like this. Stone soup for your mind. With fresh and healthful contributions from the world's great thinkers. When you fill the scrapbook, start another. Make it an ongoing project. Work toward a "best of" edition, years down the road.

#29

FEED ON
WORDS

Get yourself a good dictionary, the best and biggest you can afford. And buy (or build) a nice wooden stand that will keep the dictionary open all the time.

Place this treasure on your desk.

Read the dictionary often. The loose words will inspire you to join some together.

RECOMMENDED READING

Two of the best:

The Random House Dictionary of the English Language *is a big unabridged and brilliant reference book that contains "A Basic Manual of Style" to help you with punctuation, word usage, formatting, and proofreader's marks. It also includes foreign language dictionaries and an atlas.*

The other is The American Heritage Dictionary of the English Language. *It includes well-written definitions and wonderful illustrations.*

#30

30

SUBSCRIBE TO
MAGAZINES

In the following order, read: *The New Yorker*, *Vanity Fair*, *Esquire*, *The Atlantic Monthly*, *The New York Times Book Review*, *The Nation*, *Writer's Digest*, *The Times Literary Supplement*, *Publishers Weekly* (expensive!), *Time*, *Newsweek*, *Rolling Stone*, *Playboy*, *People*, *The Writer's Chronicle*. And a quality literary review like *The Iowa Review* or *The Paris Review*.

If anyone asks what to get you for your birthday or Christmas, tell them you want a subscription to one of these.

Peruse every issue when it arrives. Tear out excerpts you want to keep. In these pages you will see work by our finest contemporary writers, reviews of current books, surveys of the publishing market, and guidelines for writers. Such magazines are indispensable. Study them.

But limit your time. Don't let reading sessions go longer than your writing sessions.

#31

RULE # 31

CARRY A
CAMERA

If on your journey through life you're struck by a beautiful or provocative scene and there's not enough time for notes, take a picture. Painters are notorious for keeping cameras close by, so they may capture inspiring images to transfer to canvas later. Since you're a painter in words, do the same.

On research expeditions, photos are essential. Shoot indoor or outdoor settings and people—faces in particular—to help with environment and character sketches.

A small backpack can serve as your portable desk, like a kit a scientist might take into the field. Include a camera, the book or books you're currently reading, your notebook, several pens, glasses (if necessary), and a pocket dictionary.

Place your research photographs on the walls around your desk. You may be surprised to see your imagination extract from a single shot a narrative fragment or a full-blown story.

WRITE AS
THERAPY

An ancillary benefit of writing creatively, besides the joy of crafting fine sentences, is that it gives you purpose and process. You're engaged in a fascinating exploration of intellect and emotion. One manuscript ends, another begins.

It's also the best way to educate yourself. Want to learn the history of the Peloponnesian War, how to fix your car, what vegetables you can grow in a backyard garden, how to lose weight, climb the corporate ladder, buy a house, or meet interesting people? Write a book about it.

Beyond producing creative work, writing can help purge angst. You're guaranteed in life to have enemies cross your path. If someone cheats you, swindles, naysays, humiliates, or does anything short of physical harm—in other words, he zings you with language—write the guy a vicious letter. Categorize his faults, his misshapen nostrils and pallid skin. Make fun of his clothes, posture, breath, pomposity. Write a curse upon him. Explain in your most reasoned prose how he has misjudged you. List the abuses and defend yourself on each of these points. Then tear up the letter or burn it ceremoniously. There's no need to send the letter. You've expressed your viewpoint, and now it's done. He's worth no more of your time.

Success soothes better than payback. Write your way out of the sphere of your enemy's influence. Transcend such pettiness with pure art. Be great on your own. Writing gives you that option.

Jackie Collins has on her sofa an embroidered pillow that reads, "Bestsellers are the best revenge." She's had her enemies, still does. But she defeats them indirectly with her work.

Don't keep a diary wherein you record your deepest, most intimate and secret thoughts. Someone will find it and read it. Guaranteed. Do keep a journal for sketches, notes, and for practice, which is the most pragmatic of all therapies.

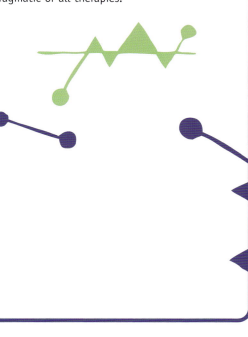

RULE # 33

THINK OF
WRITING AS
A HOBBY

The best part about writing as a hobby is the mindset. What you create is just for fun, its motive a pure childlike fascination with constructing something you're proud of, something to show your mom and dad.

There's a strange tale about a big city bookshop that hired a struggling writer to create notes for its clientele. If customers wanted a love poem, say, or a wedding toast, query letter, or an anecdote to spice up a speech, they would ask the writer for help. The bookshop manager cleared out the large bay window facing the street and put there a desk, and a sign: WORKING WRITER FOR HIRE.

The scene created a sensation. Lots of folks came by just to see the writer in the window. The more he worked on their requests the better he got, and he found out why. He had regular hours, a comfortable place to write, and he was surrounded by books to use for inspiration. But, most importantly, his craft was on display. So he replicated the arrangement as best he could at home. He put a table by his apartment window, and in the evening hours worked there on his own manuscripts. Passersby in the street saw him writing and soon asked to see what so engaged him. Every morning, he posted on a bulletin board downstairs a page he'd written the night before. Thus he completed a novel in a year, sold it, and quit the bookshop. He attributed his success to a shift in focus. Instead of thinking in grand schemes calculated for an abstract national market, he worked only on short installments meant to immediately gratify local readers, people he knew, who were watching him as he wrote. In this way he provided for himself all the conditions that help a hobbyist hone his skills, and he mastered his craft in the process.

Set yourself up like this, where your work is somehow constantly on display, and the expectations of others will help drive and refine your output.

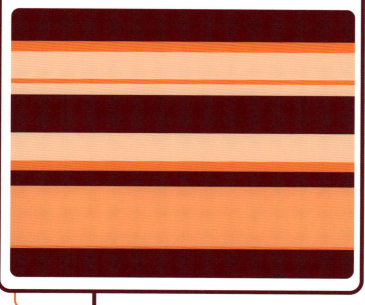

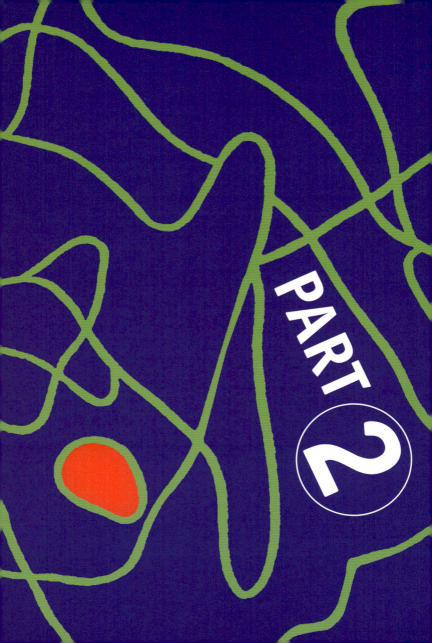

PART **2**

LANGUAGE

BUY AND STUDY A GRAMMAR **BOOK**

Listen. You can't say "between you and I" or "for you and I." It's always "between you and me," "for you and me." The problem must have begun back in the '50s and '60s when moms corrected their kids' English with, "It's you and I. You and I are going to the store. Not you and me."

The difference is that one's nominative, the other objective. If the phrase works as the subject of a sentence, it's "you and I." But if it's an object, a direct object or object of a preposition, it's "you and me." Test a sentence by taking out "you." "The fire warmed I." "That message is for I." "For" is a preposition, and its object (for whom?) has to be "me."

Yeah, yeah. You're bored already. A discussion of grammar sounds like this, and therefore only academicians and pedants find it fascinating. The abstract vocabulary alone—with terms like appositive, predicate, modifier, transitive and intransitive, parsing, syntax, imperative, subjunctive—makes most people recoil.

Grammar is the least exciting necessity of the craft. Writers begrudge it in the same way house builders begrudge the tedium of foundation work. Does it really matter if we know a gerund from a participle?

Not really, but dangling modifiers make you appear slovenly and uneducated, offer the opportunity for confusion, and may get you rejected by a strict editor.

So take a little time to get better acquainted with the English language, the medium of your art.

Many good grammars are available on the market. Try one of these: *The Little, Brown Handbook*; *The Blair Handbook*; *The Prentice Hall Guide for College Writers*; Diana Hacker's *A Writer's Reference*; *Hodges' Harbrace Handbook*; and *The Scott Foresman Handbook for Writers*.

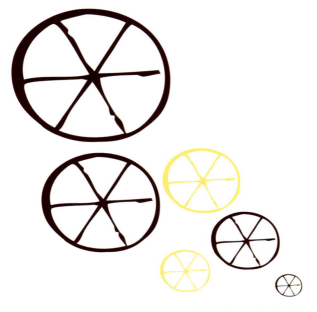

MASTER
METAPHOR

John Gardner was attacked once by a critic who claimed that if you took the word "like" away from the author, his prose would disintegrate. The charge was that Gardner, who wrote the impressive *Grendel*, *The Sunlight Dialogues*, *Nickel Mountain*, and *The Wreckage of Agathon*, relied too heavily on figurative language, particularly similes (which use "like" or "as" to make their comparisons).

Gardner's power as a storyteller—despite what that critic said—does depend largely on his use of metaphor, an observation that can be made of most successful writers.

Umberto Eco, in *The Island of the Day Before*, calls metaphor "the supreme figure of all," and defines it as "connecting remote notions, and finding similitude in things dissimilar." He goes on to say that:

> *... metaphor is the only one capable of producing wonder, which gives birth to pleasure. And knowing how to conceive metaphors, and thus to see a world immensely more various than it appears to the uneducated, is an art that is learned. For I must tell you, in this world where today all lose their minds over*

many and wondrous machines, I construct
Aristotelian machines that allow anyone to
see with words.

Metaphor permeates language and accounts for its richness. Such phrases as "the evening of life" for old age and "the golden chariot" for the sun, offer the reader a depth of observation imbued with mythical undertones.

Here's a sentence packed with figurative language:

A guy rolls into a bar, he's juiced already—got a
blazing nose, peppermint eyes—and he bellows at
the suds wizard, "Give me a St. Pauli Girl!"

Twenty-eight words, twelve of which communicate some kind of metaphor, to wit: The man rolls, but he doesn't have wheels. He's juiced but not a fruit. His nose isn't on fire, it's red from alcohol. He doesn't have candy eyes. He's not a bellows. The bartender dispenses beer, not magic with soap. And the drunken customer wants at least one more beer before he meets a real girl.

Eco claims that genius and learning consist of making metaphor. When you apply the delights of this element of craft, your stories will surely "produce wonder."

Here's one more excellent example of metaphor, this time from Pamela Bell's *The Floating City*:

The body floated past the ephemeral mansions of
the sugar barons, which were always painted white,
topped with cupolas that twisted like spun sugar,
where a lonely woman in a white dress waited on
an upper balcony, a woman who had married sugar,
and was now drowning under the weight of it.

RULE # | **36**

BUT TRY NOT TO OVERDO IT

Beware of contrived lyrical embellishment and fluffy metaphors. Write purple prose and you accomplish the opposite of what you intended, which is to create beauty.

"Her eyes were the color of the bluest sky, and I was merely a cloud passing through. Every window on the street winked and whispered the miracle of our love." The first sentence in this paragraph romanticizes a cataract; the second presents a row of cartoon-faced houses ghoulishly transposing mouths and eyes.

In Shakespeare's time there was a convention of chivalric poetry, inspired by new translations of the Song of Solomon, that featured overwrought praise. The Bard simultaneously made fun of the sappy metaphors these poets used *and* complimented his mistress with a straightforward declaration of love in the popular "Sonnet 130" by crafting lines like, "My mistress' eyes are nothing like the sun."

Wouldn't you rather be an honest, hard-working craftsman than an insufferable poser?

THE "AS" CLAUSE IS FOR AMATEURS

When "as" works as a conjunction, meaning "happening at the same time," it tends to weaken the power of the two clauses it conjoins. In other words, when "as" begins a sentence, it accelerates the reader past the information he just read and hurtles him toward what's to come, all without allowing him to savor the first clause. When the second clause begins with "as," it speeds the reader away from the first clause. Either way, the power of the two bits of information deflates.

> *As the monkey jumped from the ceiling, the rat scampered away.*

> *Beatrice saw a shark as the ship bell rang with the incoming tide.*

Fix both samples by changing the clauses to sentences:

> *The monkey jumped from the ceiling. The rat scampered away.*

> *Beatrice saw a shark. The ship bell rang with the incoming tide.*

You should avoid using "as" clauses except when absolutely necessary.

As we sharpened our swords, we became bolder.

Hit "find" on your computer, type in "as," and do a global search for its usage in your work. When the clauses are strong, revise and give them their own independent sentences, or use the coordinating conjunction "and."

Think about it. How often do you use "as" clauses in conversation? "As we walked into the store, we saw the book." Would you talk like this? It sounds affected. No, you'd say, "We walked into the store, and we saw the book."

Write like you talk.

#38

38

AVOID CLICHÉS AND STOCK PHRASES

These things are so shopworn they're useless.

An editor might let you get by with one, very deep, in a two hundred-page manuscript. Any more and you're rejected.

As big as a house. As small as a mouse.

Thick as a brick. Make it stick.

Holy cow. And how. That's good chow.

Too many examples of clichés will make you sick as a dog. If a reader can anticipate how you're going to end a phrase, you're dead in the water.

Sweet dreams are made of this.

Who am I to disagree?

You travel the world and the seven seas.

Annie Lenox of the Eurythmics strung together four clichés to begin a song and somehow managed a hit. It was the melody and beat, the contrapuntal electronic piano maybe, that offset the trite language. You have only words. Don't combine them in predictable ways.

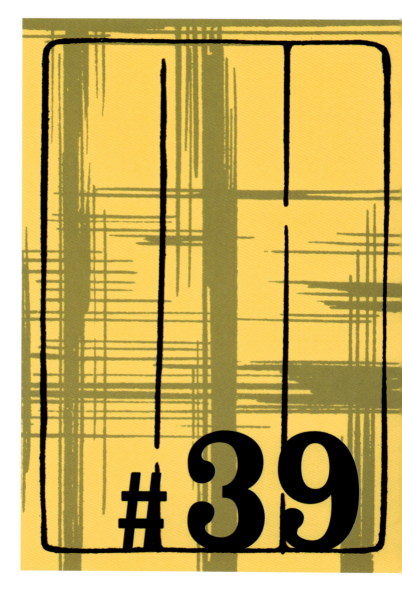

#39

TRUST THE PRECISION OF YOUR NOUNS AND VERBS

Hemingway once said about adjectives, "When in doubt, don't." Same goes for adverbs.

A big school bus rounded the corner.

"You're a jerk!" she snapped angrily.

In both sentences above, remove the modifiers. Most school buses are the same size, so "big" means nothing. And we don't need to be told that "snap" reflects anger.

Some writers recommend that you almost never use these linguistic crutches, that you always pick words strong enough to stand alone. But it's fun to see unusual modifiers. Be inventive.

A stand-by creative exercise asks writers to list words that describe, say, a sunset. The purpose is to run through the obvious: beautiful sunset, glowing, fiery, shimmering, golden. Only after you've exhausted these common adjectives will you begin to approach fresh ones: liquid sunset, calculated, poached.

Adjectives and adverbs are often forms of excessive manipulation, superfluous deductions made for what the author assumes are stupid readers. Trust your audience.

40

DON'T OVERUSE
NEGATIVES

Yes, you see the contradiction in those three words, but the rule is written that way so you won't forget. Negatives have their place sometimes, to create a dark mood or contradictory tone. But remember that the psychological effects of "no" are cumulative. They build subliminally and can wear down the audience.

These two versions of the same scene illustrate the concept:

1

No one wanted to visit Calder, particularly not in winter. He didn't need them anyway. Not a day passed without his thinking, "I won't leave this house no matter who doesn't come tracking through the field."

2

The folks kept well away from Calder. He liked being alone, especially in winter. Every day that brought silence and untouched snow was the purest blessing, and he would say, "Thank Jesus I'm rooted in the purity of my isolation."

You get basically the same tone and information in both paragraphs, although it may be argued that Calder's quotes have him more educated in the second. The first contains seven negatives (no, not, didn't, not, won't, no, don't; weighed down further by "without"), and the second has none, unless you're a player of word games and see one embedded in the word "snow."

Try to shift your text, when you can, to a positive tone. It's usually easy:

She can't take it with her.	She can leave it here.
No one wanted him to lose.	Everyone wanted him to win.
Be careful not to do it too often.	Be careful to do it only when it works.

That last pair of examples could refer to your application of the rule.

Test your negatives. If you can revise them into positives, the text will project more light than darkness and will actually energize your readers.

RULE # **41**

BE MINDFUL
OF YOUR
DICTION

Make your word selections with care. A single word, like a drop of iodine in a gallon of water, can change the color of your entire manuscript.

Much about this rule follows common sense. Change the word "water" in the above paragraph to "wine" (or gallon to galleon), and the image fails.

> *Two armor-clad knights in medieval England address each other, and one says, "Howdy."*

> *Polynesian voyagers discover the most remote islands on earth, where the beaches look like pure gold.*

> *A messenger who arrives at the field general's tent is thought to be the harlequin of victory.*

The faux pas committed in these sentences are pretty obvious. "Howdy" is for cowboys; ancient Polynesians had no knowledge of the planet Earth, nor of any metals, especially gold; and the messenger should be a "harbinger."

Review your sentences with care. Challenge each word. Is it the best choice for your meaning?

Remember, action verbs are better than the be verb (is, are, was, were)—the killer be. Crash, sing, hack, juice, spin, chop, fire your language. But pick the right word, le mot juste—e.g., watch means one thing, look another, peer something else, and then there is see, observe, study, eye, spock, gander, spot, glance, stare.

The difference between the almost right word and the right word is really a large matter—'tis the difference between the lightning-bug and the lightning.
—Mark Twain

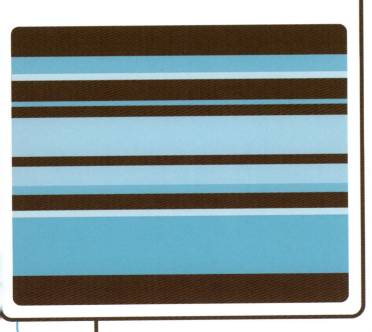

#42

AVOID REPEATING WORDS THAT SOUND OR LOOK SIMILAR

Words that are identical in sound, like tale/tail, which/witch, knight/night, sleigh/slay, wood/would are called homonyms. If they're in close proximity to one another, their music will be lost.

The same goes for homographs, words that are spelled the same but differ in meaning and maybe pronunciation. "The soldier threatened to desert in the desert."

Reading aloud will help you catch most of the similar sounds, and close line edits should prevent repeating structural groupings like, for example, using the words onion, lion, nation, ionize, elation, minion, and dictionary in the same short paragraph.

Keep your words as varied as the scenes they depict.

PLAY WITH
WORDS

Will word play make you a better writer? Absolutely. It sharpens the wit and gives you practice with metaphor.

Do crossword puzzles. Invent spoonerisms. Write acrostics. Make up riddles. Write jokes. Create definitions:

> *Pretense: stage fright*
>
> *Comeuppance: slacks cut too short*
>
> *Commentator: a regular spud*

Write down gripes about how other people use language, especially broadcasters. For example, aren't you tired of hearing sports commentators say, "He makes it look easy"? An athlete has hit a home run, surfed a double barrel at Pipeline, caught a 90-yard touchdown pass, and the man says, "He makes it look easy." It is easy. These obsessed sportsmen and women have practiced their moves over and over again until it's easy for them. Easy as walking for normal folk. They do it all the time. (By the way, you should write so much that someone says that line about you.)

Here's a thought. If someone says, "I like it," and you say, "So do I," then how come when someone says, "I don't like it," you don't say, "So don't I"?

Write down and collect these little oddities. You never know when you might use them. At worst you can bundle them into an e-mail package to send to your friends. The first duty of a writer is to entertain.

Also, type key words from your collection (acrostics, riddles, etc.) into a search engine and track resources for word games.

RECOMMENDED READING

Brain Droppings *by George Carlin. This isn't a book. It's a box of fire that will burn away all the dead wood your teachers stuffed into your head. Buy it and memorize the good parts. Caveat emptor: There are cuss words and references to sex acts in it. Carlin is not for the squeamish.*

Try www.oxymoronlist.com. This will get you thinking differently about how lame some of our terms are: uninvited guest, dry lake, first annual, bittersweet, half empty, associate head coach, authentic replica, business ethics, open secret, honest politician, nondairy creamer, mercy killing, holy war.

The Devil's Dictionary *by Ambrose Bierce. A classic, full of funny and profound definitions. For example: INFIDEL, n. In New York, one who does not believe in the Christian religion; in Constantinople, one who does.*

COLLECT GOOD TITLES AND PRACTICE WRITING **YOUR OWN**

The title might be the last thing you add to a manuscript, but it's the first thing anyone sees of your writing. As such the title constitutes an advertisement for your skills.

It's also a sign—a signal-fire brighter than those merely flickering titles—and a promise to readers that here is a book worthy of their time, a bit of brilliance to light their way.

When you're trying to come up with your own titles, keep these points in mind:

- **Oxymoronic.** Try placing into juxtaposition words that truly don't belong together: hot ice, black light; or larger phrases: sinking in granite, dawn at midnight, truth from politicians. *Way of the Peaceful Warrior* is an oxymoronic title. So is *Little Big Man*.

- **Poetic.** The sounds of words or their rhythms may excite us: *Robota. Angela's Ashes. Jabberwocky.* Beyond its fascinating meaning, the title *The Sailor Who Fell From Grace With the Sea* contains the music of an iamb followed by an anapest, another iamb, and another anapest.

- **Clichés.** Twist around or play with clichés or overly familiar phrases, taking something we've all heard before and making it different: *And the Thought Plickens*. *Pay It Forward*. *Honor Among Steves*.

- **Thematic.** These titles are the ones that entice us with those basic categories that all humans are interested in: sex, violence, money, religion, health, politics, race, environment, travel, and art. Some examples: sex—*Delta of Venus*; violence—*The War of the Worlds*. Titles that combine more than one of these thematic flags are stronger. *The Happy Hooker* is health, money, and sex. *The Battling Bibles*, violence and religion.

- **Phrases.** Ordinary phrases might surprise us as titles because they go against the popular preference for glamorous language: *Drive, He Said*. *Dude, Where's My Car?* *What We Talk About When We Talk About Love*.

- **Classics.** Look for titles embedded in lines of previous works, as John Steinbeck did with that stunning phrase from "The Battle Hymn of the Republic": *The Grapes of Wrath*. Shakespearean lines have yielded many memorable titles: *Brave New World*; *The Sound and the Fury*. And the Bible: *Blessed Are the Peacemakers*; *Inherit the Wind*.

One note of caution: Stay away from abstractions. Malice, for example, is a terrible title because it could apply to almost any story. Sometimes two abstractions put together can sound grand, and this might work: *The High and the Mighty*. *The Agony and the Ecstasy*. But if you can hook a concrete image to an abstraction, you have a better chance: *Field of Dreams*.

As with other bits of your writing, test the market. Ask your friends what they think, and then watch their eyes. If their eyes fill with light, it means you've raised their expectations, and they're returning this joy with a tough assignment for you: Write a book as good as that title.

#45

BE BRIEF

Hemingway's first editor at the *Kansas City Star* gave him this style sheet: "Use short sentences. Use short first paragraphs. Use vigorous English. Be positive, not negative." Hemingway later referred to that list as "the best rules I ever learned for the business of writing."

The last sentence on his style sheet got covered in Rule 40, and "vigorous English" is championed throughout this book. The first two points are most interesting. One says to use short sentences, but not always. Maybe it should read, "Use shorter sentences." Cut away superfluous words.

As for short first paragraphs, they are preferred for the same reason that you want a chunk of white space on your opening page: More space equals easy reading. Short paragraphs trick the reader into happily moving along. Notice this effective strategy in newspaper columns, lots of tiny paragraphs.

Brevity produces vigorous English. As Joe Friday used to say, "Just the facts, ma'am."

FOR SPEED IN COMMUNICATION, WRITE CLEARLY

Remember, you're not building a rocket ship, you're composing a book. Given the choice between elaborate, complicated expression, and straightforward clarity, go with clarity. It's easier, and it will get you a wider audience.

It's true that artists like James Joyce, Thomas Pynchon, Annie Proulx, and Cormac McCarthy have scored hits with difficult prose styles.

Take Joyce, for example. When the Modern Library judges, who named his *Ulysses* the greatest novel of the twentieth century, were asked if they had actually read the book, virtually all confessed they had not. Why? Although it's apparently the work of transcendent genius, it's so hard to read that most people simply give up on it out of boredom or sheer exhaustion. It's a great story, as *The Reader's Guide to Ulysses* will explain to you, but it's so overwhelmed with writerly flourishes it has to be excavated to be understood. Joyce forgot that all-important rule: Write to entertain. *Ulysses*, though well written, just isn't any fun.

If the writing gets in the way of the story, it's neglecting its purpose. The black marks on the white paper will be nothing more than a cleaning solution, making themselves and all they touch transparent. Instead of seeing the writing, you see what's written about.

> *We have to read a great book more than once to realize how consistently good the prose is, because the first time around, and often even the second, we're too involved in the story to notice.*
> —B.R. Myers, "A Reader's Manifesto"

#47

47

ACCELERATE THE PACE
WITH "INVISIBLE
WRITING"

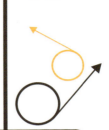

John Saul tells a great story about invisible writing. Saul is a best-selling author for two reasons: First, because kids suffer and die in his books. And second, because of pacing. The narrative races. His secret is "invisible writing," a strategy he illustrates with a story about the time he spent all day composing a description of a building. His editor loved the writing but told him to cut the paragraph. Her question: "How does this relate to the plot?" Saul bargained and got to keep half, but then the copy editor cut the remaining passage. "It doesn't forward the plot," he said. Lesson learned. The novel read better without it.

Pacing is word count. Minimum word count.

Invisible writing delivers just the bare essentials. Saul's readers had to find out what strange episodes occurred in the building; its architecture mattered only as a reflection of that strangeness. Saul wrote about "a glittering highrise," "out of place" in Boston, and the readers provided the structure in their imaginations, allowing the text to rush forward with pure narrative.

To quicken your pace, you trim the physical detail, avoid analysis, and stick to action.

RULE # 48

VARY SENTENCE STRUCTURE AND TYPE

Declarative and interrogative sentences. Simple, compound, complex, and compound-complex sentences. Fragments. Description, narration, exposition, dialogue. So many choices.

Words are the ingredients. How you measure and combine them are as important as the words themselves.

Usually, the natural rhythms of speech will take care of variety. But when you undertake line edits and read aloud, you may spot a repeated structure, long strings of prepositional phrases, or sentences that run the same length. These will blunt your rhetoric.

Readers tire of repetition. Most of the time, they'll register the literary gaffes only subliminally, but you must be able to identify what could wear down your audience, and fix it.

Let's examine a paragraph from Ursula Le Guin's The Earthsea Trilogy series. This selection runs eight sentences:

> *(1) The boat rounded a short promontory, and he saw on the shore what he took for a moment to be a ruined fortress. (2) It was a dragon. (3) One black wing was bent under it and the other*

stretched out vast across the sand and into the water, so that the come and go of waves moved it a little to and fro in a mockery of flight. (4) The long snake-body lay full length on the rock and sand. (5) One foreleg was missing, the armor and flesh were torn from the great arch of the ribs, and the belly was torn open, so that the sand for yards about was blackened with the poisoned dragon-blood. (6) Yet the creature still lived. (7) So great a life is in dragons that only an equal power of wizardry can kill them swiftly. (8) The green-gold eyes were open, and as the boat sailed by, the lean, huge head moved a little, and with a rattling hiss, steam mixed with bloody spray shot from the nostrils.

Count the words. The first sentence has 23, the second only 4. The third has 40 words, the fourth 12. Then 36, 5, 18, and 32. Le Guin consciously balanced short and long sentences.

But unconsciously she also employed different kinds of sentences: (1) compound-complex, (2) simple, (3) compound, (4) simple, (5) compound, (6) simple, (7) complex, (8) compound-complex.

She also mixes description, narration, and exposition. Mostly this is a descriptive paragraph, a picture of the dragon. Action is limited, and exposition is positioned next to images.

Provide in your manuscript such an assortment, a medley of surprising elements, and reading it will be pure joy.

Check your pages for variety in sentences, particularly their lengths. Try breaking long sentences into short ones, and conjoining short into long to see how the new arrangements balance. Shorter is preferred. But too many short sentences may chop the flow.

RECOMMENDED READING

For more such models of excellence, read Le Guin's The Earthsea Trilogy *(a fourth book has since been added), as well as* The Left Hand of Darkness.

RULE # 49

BE INTERESTING WITH EVERY SENTENCE

John Cheever reached his lofty status as our greatest short story writer (he's been called the American Chekhov for his mastery) by following this rule. It presents a daunting but simple challenge. No transitions. Each sentence should lock the readers' eyes to the page. Look at this example from Cheever's "The Swimmer":

> This was at the edge of the Westerhazys' pool. The pool, fed by an artesian well with a high iron content, was a pale shade of green. It was a fine day. In the west there was a massive stand of cumulus cloud so like a city seen from a distance—from the bow of an approaching ship—that it might have had a name.

Is there a trick to it? Sure. You write to provoke curiosity, to introduce something new. Think of the first sentence as a Russian doll. You open it, there's another doll inside, hand-painted like the first, but different—different face, more colorful costume. Each sentence opens to another. And so it continues, doll after doll after doll, deeper into the story. Make the reader wonder where it will end, what the final doll will look like.

RULE # **50**

THE DISCIPLINE OF
POETRY WILL SHARPEN
YOUR SENTENCES

A thorough course in prose must begin with poetry.

Richard Brautigan, whose work features some very good titles—*The Pill Versus the Springhill Mine Disaster*, *Loading Mercury With a Pitchfork*—began his career writing poems because, he said, "I needed to learn how to write a sentence." He became a famous poet, and then surprised his readers by switching to fiction. His explanation: "As soon as I learned how to write a sentence, I wrote a novel."

You must learn to write a sentence—or relearn it, as the case may be—and as soon as that happens you can start your book. The ideal place to practice writing sentences is with poetry.

Poetry's value is that it teaches in short bursts. It forces you always to consider the upward swing toward climax, not only in sentences, but also in phrases and lines. As a poem grows, where you break your lines will give you a sense of what elements keep the reader's eye moving down the page.

We should first agree upon a useful definition of poetry, a task even the best poets have struggled with.

Simonides, an ancient Greek, explained that, "Painting is silent poetry, and poetry is painting with the gift of speech." Wordsworth called poetry "emotion recollected in tranquillity," and "the language of men speaking to men." According to T.S. Eliot, "Genuine poetry can communicate before it is understood." William Carlos Williams believed that poetry "doesn't declaim or explain, it presents." Robert Frost: "Poetry is a way of taking life by the throat."

As you can see, most definitions of poetry are too poetic to be of much use.

Scholars tell us that poetry appears in verse form, meaning in lines instead of paragraphs, and that it employs condensed phrases and lyrical imagery. Poetic elements abound in quality prose as well, because by its nature poetry refuses to be contained. It may show up anywhere.

So what is it?

Poetry is the language of surprise.

That means "surprising language," a combination of words so original that it provokes wonder, an almost unimaginable perception of joy.

Does poetry have to make sense?

It does, but might sound like it doesn't. At least at first glance.

The best poems are much less than 100 percent poetry. They rely on the vernacular, on ordinary speech, the way flowers rely on stems and dirt. The most successful poetry is disarmingly conversational in tone.

Do practice your skills within this short, explosive genre. Read contemporary poetry and imitate it; compare your work to that of the masters, and keep revising until you're as good as they are.

SENTENCES ARE WRITTEN LIKE JOKES: THE PUNCH LINE IS AT THE END

Every sentence will contain power words, and those words should appear in the power position—the end. Check your writing for sentences that fizzle out. Chances are the stronger words are in the middle. Rearrange the sentence elements so your power words appear where they belong. Sentences should begin at a high point, dip down, and then ascend to climax.

Here's a test. Rewrite the following sentence:

The pirate found eight perfectly cut deep red rubies at the bottom of a treasure chest.

The words "red rubies" deserve climactic placement. One rewrite option is to move the prepositional phrase to the beginning:

At the bottom of a treasure chest, the pirate found eight perfectly cut deep red rubies.

The problem with this solution is that you're supposed to begin with a word or phrase that grabs attention; and "the pirate" does that much better than "at the bottom of a. ..." Also, this could be interpreted as having the pirate in the chest because prepositional phrases should be attached to the word they describe. So:

> *The pirate found, at the bottom of a treasure chest, eight perfectly cut deep red rubies.*

Notice that the new structure of the sentence heightens suspense. What the pirate found is more important than where he found it. Unless the treasure chest itself can be turned into something more wondrous than the rubies, in which case you may rewrite the sentence to read:

> *The pirate found eight perfectly cut deep red rubies at the bottom of a treasure chest made of human bones.*

The structure is the same in the last two revisions. Each sentence begins at a high point, dips down and loses steam, then ascends to climax. In the second one, the rubies are nice, but a chest made of bones is infinitely more startling.

Do remember that Rule 55: Write Like You Talk supersedes everything. If your revisions sound unnatural, with arrangements a person would never use in natural conversation, try again.

WRITE TOWARD CLIMAX

A bit of creation is a moment in time, the point of a sequence that ticks down to a clarion wake-up call. With sudden light.

Every climax explodes.

But it cannot exist unless you set the spark with a less flashy but brilliant intro, followed by a swing that provides power, and then the final delivery on the promise of an archetypal graph. All art is mathematics and chemistry.

Study the figures below. Such curves exist in nature as weapons and seeds, and they apply to most units of writing—phrases, clauses, sentences, paragraphs, sections, chapters (a cliffhanger is a climax), and poems. Even a denouement (see Rules 64 and 65) ends with a climax.

Trace the lines (easy to remember, easy to follow):

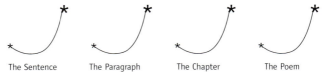

| The Sentence | The Paragraph | The Chapter | The Poem |

Curious how these identical graphs have the appearance of fishhooks, with the sparkling bait on one end, the upward curl to hold you fast, and the knotted line at the top that represents the splash of light beyond. Against gravity, fear, and darkness, this ancient contraption has the power to pull us into another world. For fish it means death, for readers rebirth. We want to be hooked and reeled in by a skilled writer.

As you create your manuscript, you will anticipate (in your imagination) a climactic image, idea, or turn of phrase coming up. Or there may be one that stands out in the draft as you read over it. Be sure to arrange and rearrange your text to feature these bright tropes. Such golden elements demand the ultimate position. They'll make you say things like, "Wow. This is so good I should end the paragraph here."

THE FIRST DUTY
OF THE WRITER IS TO
ENTERTAIN

This should probably be Rule 1, except that it's so blatantly obvious. Notice that several of these rules advise that you begin with a blaze of attention-getting rhetoric. That's what this rule is about too.

Those hooklike graphs in Rule 52 illustrate the importance of a scintillating start. Inevitably, what follows will fade by comparison. It has to. You can't sustain such glory, or you'll blind your readers. Besides, variety and contrast fuel the brightest displays of talent and heighten anticipation for the next full-on charge.

But, please, do write to entertain. That's your primary function.

Discourse on virtue and they pass by in droves. Whistle and dance the shimmy, and you've got an audience.
—Diogenes

Your secondary function is to teach. Yes, "discourse." Without being boring.

Writers are teachers. They have great lessons in life to communicate. Good teachers understand the tricks of being showmen in front of a class. They write on the board, employ props, move around, clap their hands, ask questions, mimic strange voices—whatever it takes to get their students to face front and listen.

Start with a show instead of a dry lecture. That's what Diogenes was saying. Also, take note of his command of structure. Flip-flop the positions of his sentences, and the quote loses power—it would have the people passing by at the end instead of gathering around to hear what's up. The climax for Diogenes was the reward of an audience.

Given the choice, end on a positive note.

And start with a whistle and dance. Readers lose interest with exposition and abstract philosophy. They're here because they want stories. They want to see things. Be entertained. But they will feel cheated if, in the course of entertaining, you haven't taught them something.

Remember the great dictum of Horace, who said writing must "delight and instruct." But delight first.

EVALUATING YOUR OWN WORK

As you read your work aloud, keep in mind the wisdom of William J. Martz, who said, "The words charm the ear as much as what is said charms the mind."

#54

54

TELL YOUR STORY AS FAST AS YOU CAN

> *An honest tale speeds best, being plainly told.*
> —Shakespeare, *King Richard III*

Make sure you include every detail. But hurry up. Whatever the length of your manuscript, keep the writing spare and quick.

We've all read huge books that we wish were actually bigger. *Aztec* by Gary Jennings, for example, runs a thousand pages and is so finely written we'd be happy with another thousand. Likewise for *Little Big Man* by Thomas Berger. And J.K. Rowling's increasingly thick Harry Potter books. Well written. Want more.

Notice that all these tomes have sequels. The reading public never tires of excellence.

Most books achieve their lofty reputations with concision. Not because of concision, but certainly with it; and this says something about the power of an untamed story acted out by wild characters in wilder settings. The language is frugal and direct as a result of scale.

Look at the Bible. Including "the begats." The bigger the

story, the smaller the writing. Whatever interpretations might be hung upon this scripture, it's mostly clear and easy to read.

The same goes for other sacred texts. Especially poems.

Short books may have that immense feel to them. *Ragtime*. *Heart of Darkness*. *The Rubaiyat*. Open their covers and you see a vibrant universe created by language alone, a macrocosm so vast it's barely contained, and then only by the most parsimonious of sentences.

The French have a word for it: *soigné*. It means *trim*. No wasted motion.

Speed in communication. As quickly as possible, use your writing to move the vision you have in *your* head into the head of your *reader*.

Mercury won every race because he had winged shoes that enabled him to cover great distances in fewer steps. The point is:

Create winged sentences.

EVALUATING YOUR OWN WORK

- *Can any words be cut without losing the sense of what you want to say?*

- *Will your audience understand the content of the selection easily?*

- *Does your diction lend itself to drama, with action verbs and powerful nouns?*

RECOMMENDED READING

In addition to the books mentioned above, try the first chapter of The Bean Trees *by Barbara Kingsolver. Kurt Vonnegut and Stephen King also provide excellent models. Start with Vonnegut's* Cat's Cradle *and King's* The Shining. *Also read Jerzy Kosinski's* Steps.

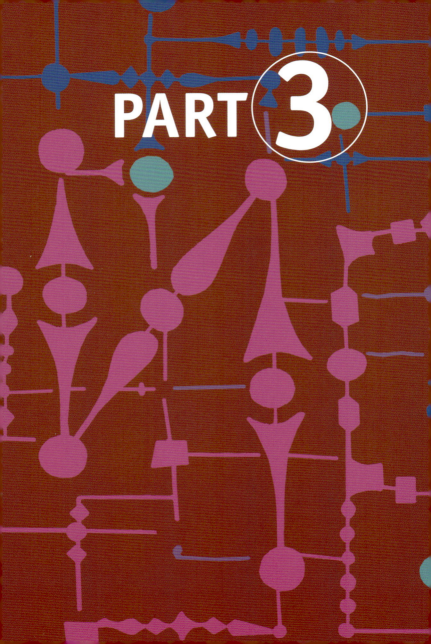

PART 3

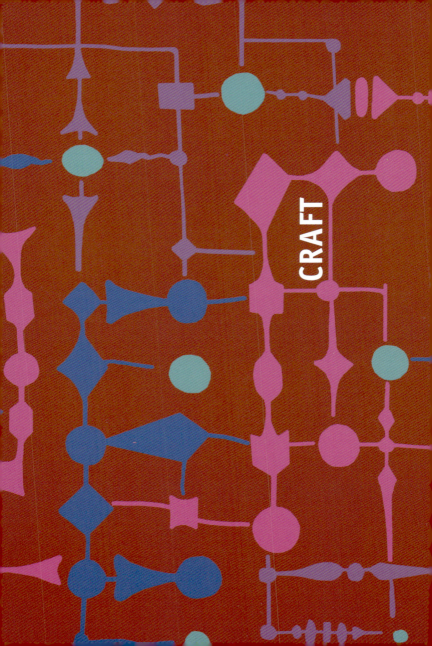

CRAFT

WRITE LIKE
YOU TALK

A good preliminary test for quality writing is to give it voice. Literally. Read your work aloud.

The ultimate test, however, and the logical extension of the concept, is to act it. Pretend you are the narrator, a one-person chorus in a play, introducing the audience to the action about to sweep across the stage. Or, more simply and realistically, that you're reciting your lines to a group of friends or business associates.

Remember when you were a kid and something you wrote was so good that the teacher felt compelled to read it to the class? That kind of writing. Fierce, immediate, and detailed.

It's like the magically performable language in children's books that turned your parents into actors. They would read aloud to you their favorite stories, usually at bedtime, and the way they read actually transported you into another world, a new way of seeing things.

What they were giving you was a model for how the written word can—and should—be made into the spoken language of a storyteller.

Whether your writing is descriptive or expository, the qualities and values of the "write like you talk" approach to the craft are key.

EVALUATING YOUR OWN WORK

Whether your text is descriptive, narrative, or expository, do the words have a conversational tone?

Does the writing sound like contrived "literature," betraying its artifice, or is it comfortable, like the regular speech of a good storyteller?

Were you self-conscious as you wrote the first draft, thinking about the quality of your "artistic expression," or were you focused instead on the subject, the story?

#56

TRUST THE POWER OF YOUR OWN VOICE

Recall those books you love, from poetry to novels to historical accounts, and think about the narrator's voice.

It's what draws you in, an establishment of trust through keen language. Think Huck Finn. Think Holden Caulfield.

Of your many concerns about the craft, the least is voice. You hear a young writer say, "I'm trying to find my narrative voice." How silly. What he just said was in his narrative voice. Write like you talk.

Or imitate someone else. You can read an author for an hour or so and experience the "imitative impulse," where the sound of that voice actually shapes the style of your thoughts. And you find that your writing may sound like whomever you're reading. Melville sounds like Shakespeare in *Moby Dick* because he was steeped in the Bard's plays at the time.

You could do worse than sounding like Shakespeare.

Your models, however, should be living writers, and we are blessed with so many first-rate stylists today. Pick one. And challenge yourself to work that well.

RULE # 57

COMMAND ATTENTION IMMEDIATELY

The first page, paragraph, sentence, line, phrase, word, title ... the beginning is the most important part of the work. It sets the tone and lets the readers know you're a skilled writer.

Most readers make snap judgments. Unless you convince them right away to read and keep reading, they'll turn to other options.

A terrific opening does more than set the tone. It puts you on a high level of artistic performance that you have to maintain, and actually improve upon.

Start right. Think of it as your last chance.

EVALUATING YOUR OWN WORK

Ask a friend or relative to listen to the way you want to begin. "I've got a story (or essay) called _____, and it opens with _____." Don't read it. Just ask if the title is catchy and the first scene compelling. If so, ask him to read and critique the first page.

DESIGN YOUR OPENING PAGE FOR MAXIMUM IMPACT

Vital elements to include on the first page of your manuscript are these: (1) the title; (2) white space; (3) a hook; (4) a sense of conflict; and (5) a cliffhanger. These basics in design and structure work to establish the integrity of your presentation and signal your skills as a professional writer.

They also have the effect of enchanting your readers, getting them to move their eyes down through the text and then to perform what every author passionately hopes for from his audience: the physical act of turning the page and reading on.

Other things take shape on page one, like point of view, the quality of your prose, and usually the setting and introduction of characters. But most important are title, white space, hook, conflict, and cliffhanger.

Your *title* should be so sharp and provocative that even though it may appear on its own "title page," you'll want to repeat it here. It also helps busy editors recall what they're reading.

Editors appreciate *white space* too, because it gives them room to take notes. More importantly, white space will trick lazy readers (aren't we all?) into thinking they don't have so much to read. It invites them in.

Now for the *hook*, a fisherman's term. We writers use it in our jargon because we are fishers too, angling to catch a reader's eye by the bone of its socket and pull it into the book. Given one chance to make a first impression, do it right. A captivating opening line can be unforgettable—"It was the best of times, it was the worst of times." "Call me Ishmael." When readers open a book, they open a world. The first sentence is a doorway *and* a path, a point of beauty that promises greater beauty ahead.

The reason we write at all is to communicate *conflict*. Nothing is more boring than people living stress-free lives. So give readers the dirt, and dish it out on page one. You don't necessarily want someone to get hit by a truck on the first page. But you must reveal at least a glimmer of evil, the talon of a hidden claw that's about to rip through your protagonist's life.

Finally, end the page with a *cliffhanger*, a moment, an action, or a break in the sentence that compels readers to keep going. Maybe a character has a gun; he cocks it. Maybe the poetry in the prose shines brightest in the last line, but you sense in the dazzle more fireworks to come.

#59

RULE # **59**

START WHERE THE STORY GETS **INTERESTING**

Surely the most self-conscious time for the writer, like a race-horse, occurs at the bell. In wanting to impress, he stumbles at the gate with a bunch of trippy sentences, disjointed logic, or too much thought presented as boring background matter.

Sometimes it isn't until the second page or so, when the story really takes over from the prose, that the quality of the writing gets better because its only function becomes the story itself. In other words, as soon as the writer thinks more about the story than the crafty ways he might tell it, he communicates most effectively.

Try this: See if you can cut or radically condense the first paragraph of your manuscript. And the second. Test how deep you can go. Where might the reader lose patience with your clumsy attempts at starting your story, and thereby lose faith in your craft? At what point? In what sentence? You may have to throw out your beginning and start later in the narrative, but such drastic cuts will make the work more engaging.

Try it.

RULE # 60

NEVER SAVE YOUR BEST FOR LAST

Poets are often guilty of finding a dream line and wanting to save it for the end of a poem. Essay writers may concoct a dazzling illustration for their core idea and position that as the climax.

But you have to ask yourself, "What is the most interesting aspect of this piece, and can I start with that?"

Open your poem with the line you're saving.

Tell at least part of that climactic episode right now.

Start with your best. Expend yourself immediately, then see what happens. The better you do at the beginning, the better you continue to do.

EVALUATING YOUR OWN WORK

Peruse your rough draft and pinpoint the most engaging sentence. If it's not on the first page, you're in trouble. Can you delete what precedes it and start here instead?

61

MASTER THE BASICS OF LITERATURE

You must pay attention to these seven basic principles for the creation of, and critical approaches to, literature: (1) quality of writing; (2) conflict; (3) point of view (POV); (4) character; (5) setting; (6) plot; and (7) theme.

They are, in order, what should occupy you as a writer. They are also, in order (pretty much), what readers track as they move through a text. Most of this book pounds the lessons of quality of writing, how to win a reader's trust with your craftsmanship. The other aspects receive in-depth treatment in their own rules. Still, a brief overview will help:

Conflict comes first. The human condition represents a set of problems. Life is tough. Everyone suffers, but we'd rather be entertained by other folks' troubles than face our own. Therefore, give your readers a sense that something's wrong. Right away. Knock them out of their comfort zone.

Point of view (POV) is the storyteller's voice. Many books are written in first-person singular, "I." The directions in these rules are third person ("he," "she," "it," "they," etc.), with the occasional use of second person, the imperative "you," and first-person plural, "we," as dictated by the conversational tone. Find a book, story, or essay that you like, and imitate the POV used by that author.

Character is the people in your story. The major players should be extraordinary, fascinating in some way. Fun to read about. Create characters similar to the ones you enjoy in literature and life. It's generally considered shrewd to add to your cast one character the reader can identify with, an Everyman or Everywoman.

Setting, where the story takes place, provides conflict and illuminates the action. Choose a well-appointed stage for your drama.

Each work of literature is a journey, and *plot* is the path your characters follow, the choreography of their steps. The gallant travelers will encounter twists, lose their way, find it again, experience a climax, and get their reward.

Finally, there must be a *theme* or moral, the lesson you're trying to teach your protagonist and, by extension, your audience.

Consider the effectiveness of all seven of these aspects as you shape your manuscript.

By the way, E.M. Forster, in his landmark book *Aspects of the Novel,* has a different list of seven: story, people, plot, fantasy, prophecy, pattern, and rhythm. The last four of these are elusive and "artsy," referring mostly to quality of writing. Fantasy, says Forster, adds the necessary ingredient of strangeness to fiction (touching on setting), while prophecy gives the tone authority, a sense of greatness (theme). Pattern expands upon plot and limits a novel to a definable shape, a condition that may begin to make unnatural demands on the narrative. Rhythm is better as Proust used it because it is as natural and flexible as music.

MIX DESCRIPTION, NARRATION, EXPOSITION, AND DIALOGUE

The first three elements of prose—description, narration, and exposition—communicate things, movement, and reason:

description = image (things)

narration = action (movement)

exposition = idea (reason)

The following sentence from O.A. Bushnell's *Ka'a'awa* is purely descriptive, so it is dominated by concrete nouns:

> *The field of grass, cropped close by the goats, was like the water of a green pond, lapping at a house standing high on stilts.*

If a writer stops the flow of the narrative and takes stock of physical details, he uses description, like a freeze-frame in a movie. Like a photograph. The scene above could be a postcard from the island of O'ahu.

When action resumes, and the movie moves again, we switch back to narrative; the dominant power words are action verbs. Look at this example from Ridley Pearson's *The First Victim*:

> *Rodriguez flew back off balance and Stevie stepped*
> *forward and kicked him in the face, feeling the bone*
> *and gristle of his nose give way.*

Narration happens in time; it is chronological, with a beginning, middle, and end. Verbs transport us along this journey.

We may stop the narration again by commenting on it. Such observations are delivered in exposition, the language of idea, as in this example from George Orwell's *1984*:

> *An example was prolefeed, meaning the rubbishy*
> *entertainment and spurious news which the Party*
> *handed out to the masses. Other words, again, were*
> *ambivalent, having the connotation "good" when*
> *applied to the Party and "bad" when applied to its*
> *enemies.*

The selection relies on abstract nouns like example, entertainment, connotation, good, bad, and enemies. We see none of these things because they are conceptual, existing only in the realm of thought. But this kind of writing is how values and judgments are delivered most economically. You tell your reader what to think.

The fourth element, just as vital to good prose, is dialogue, or the introduction into the text of what Henry James called "other voices."

dialogue = voices

Any well-written book provides useful samples of dialogue, as in this brief exchange from *The Red Tent*, by Anita Diamant:

> *"What is it, child?" she murmured, half asleep.*
>
> *"Danger," I hiccuped.*

She sat upright, and the shadow leaped down toward me. I covered my head and shrieked.

Re-nefer laughed softly. "A cat," she explained.

Are these classifications—description, narration, exposition, and dialogue—important? Should writers take time to learn them? Can't we just write without such distractions?

The answer to all three questions is yes. Tell your story naturally. But for the sake of variety, practice these four kinds of writing. Master each one (in the order presented above). You'll put your reader to sleep with huge blocks of exposition or pure narration. Mix the elements and your style will come alive.

*Variety is not just the spice of life,
it's the essence of great art.*
—Imal Desberats

63

FOR STRUCTURE, REMEMBER THE GOLDEN TRIANGLE

A triangle provides the simplest building structure. Triads serve as models in music, culture, and logic. In stories there's a beginning, middle, and end. In essays: introduction, body, conclusion. In grammar and life: past, present, and future. Father, Son, Holy Ghost; you, me, them; good, better, best; blah, blah, blah.

Three is the best organizing principle for writers.

A study of college short-form essays concluded that most of the outstanding manuscripts contained five paragraphs: an introduction, a three-paragraph body, and a conclusion.

The introduction typically consisted of three sentences. A provocative opening to hook the reader's eye. A transition that heightened drama. And the thesis statement, which appeared at the end of the first paragraph.

The body detailed each of three main points emphasized in the thesis. The conclusion (which also had three sentences) reminded the reader of the topic without actually summarizing.

Three words to remember: Speed in communication.

64

USE THE
CLASSICAL PLOT
OUTLINE

The greatest gift the Greek dramatists bestowed upon humankind was this: ascending action, climax, denouement. That very simple structure seems to have eluded some writers. Let's analyze it by defining its parts:

Ascending action is the buildup, the accumulation of difficult facts. The heightening of suspense. The learning curve. The ladder to enlightenment.

Climax is the explosion, the moment of greatest intensity. Fireworks.

Denouement (day-noo-MAHN) is the unraveling, the settling back. Resolution and reward.

Notice the lengths of each part on the graph. Ascending action takes a long time; climax is quick, a rush of glory;

and denouement short. It's like blowing up a balloon until it pops—KABLAM!—you're left with the ragged end.

People know the structure by instinct. It's wired into our brains, our very being. There are two reasons this happened, one mental and the other physical.

As humans, the most important thing we do mentally is problem solve. We attack every quandary with thought and experimentation, looking for a way to fix it. Then the solution dawns on us, and we see what to do.

It could be said that the most important thing we do physically (other than survive) is the sex act. There's the ascending action of foreplay and serious love-making; followed by the climax; and then rest, afterglow.

Now, here's what's interesting about all this. Because we understand the dramatic structure so well—know it shallow and deep, consciously and subliminally—we therefore expect it to be repeated in art.

In writing, it's the classical plot outline, and it affords a framework upon which to prop your longer stories, in-depth essays and articles, certainly novels, biographies and other lengthy narrative nonfiction, as well as film scripts and plays.

Ascending action, climax, denouement.

Deviate from it and you leave your readers unsatisfied. Apply it and you tap into emotional wells as deep and ancient as the human race.

65

A MORE DETAILED PLOT OUTLINE PROVIDES YOUR **TEMPLATE**

Your story should begin at a high point, a curiously fascinating moment. Most writers employ a device called in medias res, "in the middle of things," starting with a timeline based on preceding events.

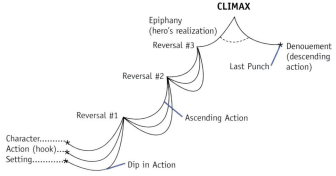

Three things happen simultaneously in this model, following the progress of character, action, and setting.

The protagonist, or main character, undertakes a journey of

self-discovery, but suffers setbacks called reversals. Traditionally there are three major ones, marking the three acts of a drama. He overcomes the last, potentially devastating setback, wins a victory, and here his world-view changes. He experiences an epiphany, and is forever afterward a changed man. In the denouement his buddies applaud his triumph.

The epiphany occurs just before or just after the climax (hence the dotted line on the chart). If before, then the hero comes into his power and causes the big boom. He pulls the trigger, lights the fuse, fires his sling-stone. If after, then the climax causes the epiphany—it takes an explosion for the guy to finally see the light.

The sweep of ascending action is a series of events that teaches our protagonist how to reach his epiphany—including the reversals that so damage him. Each problem that flares in his path is worse than the last, but they're small fires compared to the huge conflagration of the climax. Some scholars describe the dramatic arc as threads or strings, and the climax ties everything into a knot—the highest, most tension-filled point of conflict. The denouement follows, and the pitch of action descends. Just as the plot begins with a pop, the denouement concludes with a last punch: a roar from the crowd, shooting stars, some kind of benign echo of the climactic detonation.

Finally, the setting may undergo a change that coincides with and parallels the action, leading uphill, as in *Zen and the Art of Motorcycle Maintenance*, where the riders climb a mountain; or downhill, as in Dante's descent through hell in the *Inferno*. A lot of writers use the strategy of "parallel terrain" only for certain scenes.

That's how you organize the grand story you want to tell. Your employment of the plot outline may be subtler, but this scheme is vital to artistic success. It's the lodestar of creative genius.

Review the "Evaluation Guide for Writing" in the appendix; it walks you through the plot process.

RECOMMENDED READING

The Writer's Journey: Mythic Structure for Storytellers and Screenwriters, *by Christopher Vogler, neatly summarizes Joseph Campbell's theories on mythic plot structure. Also read* Writing a Novel *by John Brain. For the source, go to* The Hero With a Thousand Faces *by Joseph Campbell, and* The Power of Myth *by Joseph Campbell (with Bill Moyers).*

RULE # 66

ALLOW THE PROCESS OF DISCOVERY TO HAPPEN NATURALLY

You have a story to tell. What happens will always happen in a dramatic sequence.

A widow finds an emerald ring in her dead husband's safe. The ring is engraved with a name: Delores. The widow begins asking her friends if they've heard of this woman.

An archaeologist uncovers an ancient stone in Egypt with a carved map of what looks like a borough in New York City. He travels to the neighborhood and finds the spot marked on the stone—it's a clothing store. He goes in and meets the owner, an Egyptian man.

A couple's eight-year-old daughter is murdered. The case remains unsolved. They find handmade teddy bears with unusual black fur and red sequin eyes by her grave, and decide to hide in the cemetery to find out who's been leaving the bears.

One thing leads to the next. It's a hunt, but for what? Where will this strange trail lead? Such is the process of discovery.

Any mystery gets solved by following a string of clues. Make them interesting, and the reader will stay with you forever.

DIALOGUE HEIGHTENS DRAMA

Dialogue enhances action and often provokes it, through verbal baiting, verbal foreplay, or the process of discovery through conversation.

> *"Hit me."*
>
> *"No."*

Perfect dialogue can be as short as this. Three words. Maybe just two. Maybe you write:

> *"Mom?"*
>
> *"Hush."*

These examples of two brief lines each suggest things about the situation and the minds of the characters. Readers hear this dialogue and naturally begin to extrapolate the context.

In the first we may be watching a boxing match with a reluctant opponent. Or a game of "21" with a stingy dealer. In the second there's someone who maybe doesn't want to be identified as a mother. Or, perhaps there's an urgency that requires silence.

Notice the examples also follow the rule of magnifying conflict in dialogue. Usually dialogue should be confrontational: yes/no; he said/she said.

Dialogue also demands scenes. If you've been admonished by your writing coach to show instead of tell, try inserting dialogue into your narrative. You can't have a conversation without stopping everything—background observation, editorial commentary—to watch these people talk.

The most important feature of dialogue is that it reveals character. What the people in your story say tells readers more about them than their costumes, their physical tics, how they decorate a room, or even what they do. For fictional characters, words (in dialogue) speak louder than action.

See Emily Brontë's *Wuthering Heights* for some of literature's best confrontational dialogue. Review all these dialogue rules, and go for the gab.

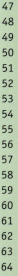

#68

RULE # **68**

DIALOGUE SPEEDS THE PROCESS OF DISCOVERY

If the characters aren't in a state of conflict, they should be on a mutual path of investigation. In the television series *The X-Files*, agents Scully and Mulder made a science of this, and creator/writer Chris Carter made a bundle:

> *"Mulder, come here. I want you to see something."*
>
> *"What is that thing?"*
>
> *"I'm not sure. What do you think will happen if I put it in the microwave?"*
>
> *"Let's find out."*

No one argues in this kind of dialogue. There's no confrontation whatsoever. In fact there's such a level of cooperation that your main character could be having a conversation with himself, his inquisitive alter-ego.

You find such exchanges common in buddy stories, and they are de rigueur in mysteries. Two people talk out a solution, verbalizing the steps of exploration.

DIALOGUE
CREATES
TENSION

Most of the time, follow the Rule of Conflict (the notion that all great literature emphasizes conflict—see Rule 84) when you write dialogue. The speakers must be arguing or sniping at each other, or else their reactions seem illogical.

Cable news shows are onto this. Network producers figured out the formula, and so should you: People are drawn by the sound of sharp words.

The program directors call it lively debate, but usually it's yelling, interruption, and bald effrontery. Whatever happened to civility and manners? They don't sell.

You must ratchet up the tension in your dialogue. Small talk never engages a reader. Study this selection from *House of Sand and Fog* by Andre Dubus III:

> "You sure about that?" The policeman turns from the wall, regarding me with a smile.
>
> I release the door and it closes quietly on its compress arm. "Are you interrogating me?"
>
> "I don't know, Colonel. You tell me. I understand

your friend the Shah used to make a real habit of it."

"I do not know who you think you are speaking to, sir, but I have had quite enough. You have done your job; now you may leave." I open the door once again, standing to its side.

The policeman walks to me. He is taller than I. He smells of garlic and charred wood.

"You're used to giving orders, aren't you, Colonel?"

Notice that the underlying motives for these two characters fuel their confrontation. You have to ask of the people in your story, "What do you want?" In Dubus's scene there's a clash of cultures, with an American cop and an Iranian immigrant. The cop wants him to give up his house. The immigrant knows his ownership is legal and is determined to stay. The cop wants to intimidate. The Iranian, a former colonel in his home country, maintains his practiced superiority. Put people with opposing desires in one room and they're bound to yell at each other.

Tension can also be accomplished by conversational misdirection, when people seem at cross-purposes. Characters can refuse to respond logically to each other and try to avoid certain issues by changing the subject. This can lead to frustration, with characters trying to steer away from the in-your-face hostility that's boiling just beneath the surface.

As your crafted conversations go on, the tension should heighten toward a climactic moment that ends with a parting shot.

USE DIALOGUE TAGS CORRECTLY

Why is it that beginners want so badly to find synonyms for said?

> *"There's a bat in the kitchen," Nita opined.*

> *"So?" responded Chuck with a shrug.*

> *"Should we get rid of it?" she queried.*

Come on. Is this the way you'd tell a scene to a friend? Literature should be no different in terms of style than plain talk. That goes double for dialogue.

> *Nita said to Chuck, "There's a bat in the kitchen."*

> *He shrugged. "So?"*

> *"Should we get rid of it?"*

Use "said" for statements, and "asked" for questions. And that's it. No exceptions. The reason is economy. Readers take as little notice of them as they do points of punctuation.

Also, place the tags within the quoted material when you can. Certainly in long quotes, and shorter ones too. For examples of this, as with all points of craft, consult the professionals. Here is a line from *The Joy Luck Club*, by Amy Tan:

"About time you got home," said Vincent. "Boy are you in trouble."

Try putting the tag at the end, and you get denouement:

"About time you got home. Boy are you in trouble," said Vincent.

Not nearly as effective. Better the way Tan has it, ending with "trouble." Let's examine another selection from *The Joy Luck Club*:

"Be careful, An-mei," she said. "What you hear is not genuine. She makes clouds with one hand, rain with the other. She is trying to trick you, so you will do anything for her."

Here it can be argued that the best part of this paragraph appears in the middle. It should be rearranged thus:

"Be careful, An-mei," she said. "She is trying to trick you, so you will do anything for her. What you hear is not genuine. She makes clouds with one hand, rain with the other."

This way that beautiful clouds/rain metaphor is the last thing we hear. It is now allowed to sing in the memory.

ESTABLISH
POINT OF VIEW
EARLY

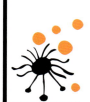

We convey information to each other every day and never think about point of view (POV). Why worry about it now? Just tell your story the way you would to a friend.

There are two basic points of view: first person and third person.

First person is "I," and the plot reveals itself through the eyes, ears, and voice of the one it happened to, "me." The challenge in using this approach lies in developing a voice with personality, like that of Jack Crabb in Thomas Berger's *Little Big Man*, or Garp in John Irving's *The World According to Garp*.

We use third person ("he," "she," "it") to tell stories about other people. Most third-person narratives in popular fiction are omniscient, meaning the storyteller knows everything, the thoughts of the characters, the past, present, and future; he has the all-knowing power of a god. Any writer who has command of his plot will know these things anyway, but with the third-person omniscient POV he chooses to let the reader in on his vast knowledge.

Some writers back away incrementally from this POV and curtail the omniscience, so to speak. This results in a third-person limited omniscient POV. Yes, that's what they call it, and nobody knows why because it's a contradiction in terms. For example, you may choose to reveal the thoughts of one or two main characters but no one else, or everyone's internal monologues but mention nothing about future events.

Some third person accounts follow just the main character. Others are like most films, wherein you witness scenes that happen among secondary characters away from the protagonist.

Few fiction authors use second person, "you," to tell a story. Mostly because it's just plain weird. Jay McInerney bucked convention and succeeded in writing a book in second person, although at times it reads like an admonishment. His novel *Bright Lights, Big City* opens in a Manhattan nightspot with the line, "You are not the kind of guy who would be at a place like this at this time of the morning."

Whatever POV you select, make it clear from the beginning. If there are multiple viewpoints, make a shift early on. In other words, you can't track just the protagonist for a hundred pages then suddenly introduce a scene without him.

Pick a point of view that seems most comfortable for you. If you're not sure, try experimenting. Rewrite a chapter or story from another POV altogether and see how that sounds. Some novelists have finished a book manuscript and then decided to switch the POV from first to third person, or vice versa. The challenges and rewards of such an exercise can be fascinating.

#72

RULE # **72**

KEEP YOUR CHARACTERS REAL

We adore eccentricity. Most of the folks who populate the real world, never mind invented ones, distinguish themselves by being unusual.

Characters might stray too far in their weirdness, however, and the rap on these books has been that some members of the cast just get too goofy. Herein lies the danger. You want strangeness within realistic bounds, psychological richness without cartoonish exaggeration. And there must be an eye in the hurricane, a regular and reasonable person much like your average reader, around whom these larger-than-life personalities swirl.

Some of the most outstanding characters—Hamlet, King Arthur, Ivanhoe, Hawkeye, Oliver Twist, Frankenstein, Dracula, Captain Nemo, Lord Jim, Stephen Dedalus, Tarzan, Gatsby—have transcended their pages to stand forth almost as archetypal figures. You need not pressure yourself into creating anyone so grand. (Or maybe you should, ambitious writer that you are.)

But the models are there. Use them. Aspire to their standard when you cast your book, and your characters will have a better chance at greatness.

RULE # 73

GIVE THE OPPOSITION QUALITY ATTENTION

Balance your protagonists with compelling antagonists.

If there are archetypal heroes, there are archetypal villains as well: Goneril (*King Lear*), Claudius (*Hamlet*), Roger Chillingworth (*The Scarlet Letter*), Inspector Javert (*Les Miserables*), Injun Joe (*Tom Sawyer*), Captain Bligh (*Mutiny on the Bounty*).

Charles Dickens proved adept at creating such memorable villains as Fagin (*Oliver Twist*), Scrooge (*A Christmas Carol*), and Uriah Heep (*David Copperfield*). Villains like Lex Luthor and Darth Vader also will continue to fascinate us for generations.

The best villain in literature remains Iago, the scheming lieutenant in *Othello*, the one Coleridge called a "motiveless malignancy." His icy machinations against his master serve as a template for willful evil.

As you devise your villains, make them psychologically complex. Create something surprising in their personalities that may even endear them to us a little. Give the opposition quality attention and good lines. Nothing is worse than a setup—making bad guys look incompetent so your heroes can triumph. The power of the antagonists should equal that of the protagonists.

74

TELL A DREAM AND YOU RISK BORING A READER

This rule applies most exclusively to fiction, narrative nonfiction, and scripts, where the writer may do one of two things. He relates a dream that a character has. Or he fools the reader into believing that some terrible incident has just taken place, and then—voila!—the person wakes up. It was only a dream.

The problem in the first instance arises because art itself is already a dream. Readers know that the world they see through your writing exists only in the mind. Moviegoers understand that they're sitting in a room watching colored light on a screen and hearing sound through speaker boxes. But the artist so effectively engages their imagination that for a moment they experience the art as reality. Just like in a dream. So when a writer drops a dream self-contained into a story, the audience is required to step through their dream and into someone else's—to experience a dream within a dream. That's a lot to ask. If dreams are important to your story, tell them piecemeal. We want to see what these characters are doing in their real lives, not slug our way through a dream sequence. But if you deliver a dream in bits, and make its telling a scene, it works better.

The second way writers annoy their readers with dreams is with the "it's only a dream" scenario. In *Aliens*, Ripley lies in a hospital, experiences pain in her chest, and watches horrified as the sheet rises with what we know is a baby alien (a "chest burster") coming out of her. Then she wakes up.

A whole season of the '80s primetime soap *Dallas* was one character's dream.

Readers can't help but feel tricked, ripped off by this manipulative device. Because that's all it is. A cheap gimmick meant to heighten suspense. Art is already fake. Readers pretend it's not, but a device like this makes it even more fake.

It's also overused. We've seen it already, and in more successful guises, as in *Total Recall* and *Memento*.

Samuel Taylor Coleridge called audience participation in drama "that willing suspension of disbelief for the moment, which constitutes poetic faith." We don't believe what we see is real, but we suspend our disbelief for the sake of enjoying the story. It's a matter of trust. Dreams betray that trust.

#75

75

SETTING
MATTERS

And now where are we? Does it matter? Always.

Setting is a romanticized and particular environment shaped by your insights and eye for detail. It's a place as malleable as clay, and you can bend and twist it to support your story.

A thunderstorm, the sky shattered with lightening, trees bowing to heavy wind, the air ozone-thick and lavender, and beneath the dark chaos a shelter—a cave or palace—its floor pooling with water from the summer deluge, its walls orange with lamplight, hail hammering the roof. ... This is setting.

Setting establishes mood. Leave nothing to the imagination. Writers who say they want to leave something to the imagination of their readers are lazy writers indeed.

Be specific, yet brief—only as detailed as the pace of the narrative allows.

Paint pictures with your words. Let the landscape on the page—rendered only in words—shine as beautifully, as remarkably, and as true as the real world your readers are trying to escape.

ALLOW FOR DESCRIPTIVE PASSAGES

In presenting description, try to mimic the tendencies of the human mind's natural curiosity.

It sets the eye upon the whole scene first, then spirals inward, as in this excerpt from *Village of a Million Spirits*, by Ian MacMillan:

> *The people kept their distance from the drunk. He was lying propped against the side of the bus stop bench, and his hands were dirty and limp, folded between his knees. The fabric of his clothes was packed with grime on the thighs of his pant-legs and around the pockets. His mouth was slack—a droplet of saliva glistened on the stubble of his chin.*

Notice how the image begins with a wide shot of a man on a bench and zooms inward to his hands, his clothes, his mouth.

Spiraling may also serve as a panorama by moving outward instead of inward as in the following example:

> *Ten geese drifted on the lake. Beyond them the pine boughs went gold in the last sunlight, and the sky turned a dusky, cloudless indigo.*

In these two scenes—the bum on the bench and the geese on the lake—the structure depends on three movements: close, closer, closest; far, farther, farthest.

Organize your descriptive passages in the most logical and natural way, and refine the details with increasing power. Transform artifice into something so authentic the reader will think he's looking at real life instead of mere words.

PRACTICE THE ELEMENTS OF DESCRIPTION

In stories, as in life, we must sometimes stop everything that's going on. Stop, and observe. For storytellers this represents a kind of crossover into visual art because here we paint word pictures, or snap photographs in phrases.

The two primary categories of descriptive writing are cata-logues and sketches. They're fairly easy to do. Invest a little in their creation and they pay back ten-fold in your narrative:

CATALOGUES

A catalogue is a list, perhaps the quickest application of detail. Usually it just names the objects, but sometimes the list becomes more involved. For example, here's an extended catalogue from *ARCTIC DREAMS: Imagination and Desire in a Northern Landscape*, by Barry Lopez:

> *The Arctic Ocean can seem utterly silent. If you low-ered a hydrophone, however, you would discover a sphere of "noise." The tremolo moans of bearded seals. The electric crackling of shrimp. The baritone boom of walrus. The high-pitched bark and yelp of ringed seals. The clicks, pure tones, birdlike trills,*

and harmonics of belukhas and narwhals. The ele-
phantine trumpeting of bowhead whales. Added to
these animal noises would be the sounds of shifting
sediments on the sea floor, the whine and fracture of
sea ice, and the sound of deep-keeled ice grounding
in shallow water.

SKETCHES

These may be of landscapes, architecture, or wildlife. But their most important subject is people. When introducing a person to your story, it's customary to provide a character sketch, which is a brief "drawing" of what this human looks like. Let's look at an example from Charles Frazier's *Cold Mountain*:

The blind man was square and solid in shoulder and
hip, and his britches were cinched at the waist with
a great leather belt, wide as a razor strop. He went
hatless, even in the heat, and his cropped hair was
thick and grey, coarse-textured as the bristles to a
hemp brush. He sat with his head tipped down and
appeared to be somewhat in a muse, but he raised
up as Inman approached, like he was really looking.
His eyelids, though, were dead as shoe leather and
were sunken into puckered cups where his eyeballs
had been.

While the images may electrify in this selection, the prose is fat and the sketch too long, especially since it describes a minor character in the novel. And that's always the danger. By all means, include description, but never allow it to slow your narrative.

#78

USE IMAGES
TO DELIVER
IDEAS

Philosophy and abstractions should be packaged and sold in gift boxes. Because concept is noncorporeal (you can't see an idea), you should place expository sentences next to descriptions.

In *The Farthest Shore*, from The Earthsea Trilogy, Ursula Le Guin does this in striking fashion in her rendering of the dragon dying on the beach:

> ... *the sand for yards about was blackened with the poisoned dragon-blood. Yet the creature still lived. So great a life is in dragons that only an equal power of wizardry can kill them swiftly. The green-gold eyes were open.* ...

Le Guin places her exposition between two of the most visual details. Her abstract sentences are pure analysis. Deduction, concept, idea. And where do we find this dry reflection? Between images.

Provide for your ideas a medium of images and stories.

79

AVOID COMMENTARY;
LET READERS MAKE THEIR
OWN DEDUCTIONS

> *Not ideas about the thing, but the thing itself.*
> —Wallace Stevens

Like his colleague William Carlos Williams, poet Wallace Stevens was a disciple of "imagism," a literary movement that flourished in early twentieth-century America and England, and which emphasized sharply delineated images. What Stevens said took the "no ideas but in things" notion one step further.

In *Sacred Wood: Essays on Poetry and Criticism*, T.S. Eliot, another poet roused by imagism, wrote a critical essay titled "Hamlet and His Problems" that provided a catchphrase for the movement:

> *The only way of expressing emotion in the form of art is by finding an "objective correlative"; in other words, a set of objects, a chain of events which shall be the formula of that particular emotion; such that when the external facts, which must terminate in sensory experience, are given, the emotion is immediately invoked.*

So: the thing itself. The image. No explanations about it. Ideas are merely implied.

English teachers love Eliot's term, "objective correlative," because it sounds so much more refined and erudite than "symbol" or "symbolic act." But that's what it means. An "object" or scene that "correlates" to an idea. Its importance isn't so much that it invites exploration into the theme, moral, or psychology of a work, but how it does so through spectacle alone.

Imagists were inspired by haiku, with its reliance on brevity and lyric detail. Ezra Pound's poem "In a Station of the Metro" has become emblematic of their stripped-down focus:

> *The apparition of these faces in the crowd;*
>
> *Petals on a wet, black bough.*

Honestly, it would be a mistake to limit yourself to the confines of strict imagism. We make observations and judgments all the time. And they can be very interesting when presented as natural developments in the surge of a storyteller's invention. But the Stevens quote gives us a most useful touchstone, as a poignant reminder of the old mantra "Show, don't tell."

When you infer rather than explain—allow objects to speak for themselves, and action to tell the story—your readers will love you for trusting them.

> *If you use the word color, it ruins the word blue.*
> —Tony Quagliano, "One for William Carlos Williams"

#80

RULE # 80

TELL THEM STORIES TO KEEP THEM READING

No matter what you're writing—be it analytical chemistry reports, environmental impact statements, or documentary strategies for the exculpation of the Nazi demimonde (falderal and fiddle-de-dee)—you can get your readers interested with a good story.

This happened and then that happened, which led up to the most amazing incident.

> *The Pierce family refused to let go of Christmas and left their tree up. It was still there in April, when the fire started.*

Essay writers know this as "the anecdotal opening." And it's the kind of tactic used to elicit a reader's trust and attention.

The trick is to know when your prose might need the rejuvenation of a quick narrative burst. Scan your entire document, looking for long passages of exposition, description, or dialogue. Do they carry on at the risk of boring your reader? If so, insert an anecdote, fable, folk tale, legend, parable, joke, any bit of storytelling art to break them up. A book can be a perpetual motion machine, but only if you pack it with the self-generating power of electrical narrative.

REVEAL PAST EVENTS THROUGH EXPOSITION OR FLASHBACK

Rookie writers often make the mistake of having characters talk about the past for the sake of the reader; rookie editors let it go, and so it still shows up in television dramas particularly, as well as in literary journals and comic books.

Here is how it happens. You write a scene of two people talking, and one refers to a past event, some vital bit of backstory, but in a way that rings false for these characters because they were involved in the incident. They review what happened not for themselves, but in order to let the audience in on it. This is a silly way to provide information about the past because it's obviously contrived and not at all like real life.

> *"I thought I'd laugh to death," Paul said, "when Grandma took her dentures out and put them on the table and a cockroach climbed on and, because her eyesight's not so good, she put them back in and never noticed a thing. But I saw that you saw it happened, Julia."*

Who would talk this way? Julia was obviously present during the famous cockroach incident and doesn't need Paul to rehash it for her.

If these two characters were relating the moment to a third party, this could work. Or if the kids had short-term memories and were helping each other out. You can actually heighten the drama by cutting dialogue down to the barest and most authentic kind of conversation (imitate real life), and then reveal what happened before the scene in plain narrative:

> "I thought I'd laugh myself to death," Paul said.
> "A stowaway cockroach!"
>
> *Their grandmother's eyesight was poor or she might have seen the roach. She had taken off her dentures and put them on the table …*

Again, let common sense guide you to the most natural way of telling your story.

SHIFT FOCUS
OFTEN

Approach your scenes like a movie director would, using multiple camera angles and quick edits.

The best way to test the veracity of this rule is to pick up a book by a highly regarded author and open it anywhere. There you'll find an example. It's really the most common way of storytelling, to present a potpourri of images.

Le Guin does it in the paragraph we saw in Rule 48. Observe the shifts and think of them as shots in a film. First there's a focus on the boat, then the shore, then the "ruined fortress" dragon, tight on its wings, one rocking in the waves. Then a tracking shot along the body, foreleg gone, shredded ribs, torn belly, bloody sand, green-gold eyes. Quick cut back to boat. Return to the dragon, tight on the head, zoom in on the nostrils.

Let's look at an example that involves only one angle:

The dragon flew in, and he had a belly of white scales, except for one spot. Here an arrow hit him, in the gap. The dragon shrieked and fell to the ground.

Now the same scene, as crafted by J.R.R. Tolkien in *The Hobbit*:

The dragon swooped once more lower than ever, and as he turned and dived down, his belly glittered white with sparkling fires of gems in the moon—but not in one place. The great bow twanged. The black arrow sped straight from the string, straight for the hollow by the left breast where the foreleg was flung wide. In it smote and vanished, barb, shaft and feather, so fierce was its flight. With a shriek that deafened men, felled trees and split stone, Smaug shot spouting into the air, turned over and crashed down from on high in ruin.

In the first paragraph, the flat focus remains on the dragon. It's one continuous shot. One angle. In Tolkien's rendering, there's a wide-angle of the dragon, followed by a tight and poetic observation of his belly, then a new shot on the earth and close-up on the bow, then a tracking shot of the arrow propelled upward, its rise and disappearance into the dragon, the aerial shriek that affects men, trees, and stone back on the ground, then up once more to the sky where the dragon turns over and crashes down in ruin.

Up, down, up, down, back and forth. What these moments accomplish, as they jump from sky to earth and up again, is the replication of shot edits in a movie. Do like Tolkien. Like Le Guin. Shift focus.

EVALUATING YOUR OWN WORK

See the writing as film. You're a filmmaker in words. That's it.

83

KNOW YOUR
THEME

In the who, what, where, when, and why of a story, the why exposes theme. It is the psychology, the developing moral, the lesson being learned by the protagonist—therefore the lesson for the reader, who participates vicariously in the action.

All themes come under broad headings: love, war, honor, duty, faith, patriotism. As you work the theme of your novel or story, you must sharpen its focus: love conquers all; war is hell; there's honor among thieves; duty obligates soldiers to obey orders; faith without works is dead.

Unlike the essay, which generally provides a thesis statement and straightforward rhetoric to communicate its concepts, fiction employs entertaining tricks.

If your theme is "saving the natural environment from pollution," your tale may feature oil-soaked birds in Prince William Sound and the people who rescue them and clean their feathers. The exhausting drama and sad detail of the scene will do more than any statistic-bloated nonfiction to educate your readers about the horrors of pollution.

Characters in your story might preach the theme, but the

authorial voice—your voice as the author—shouldn't. And whatever the preaching, it takes a back seat to what drives the story and the plot.

The power of the story should so intrigue us that we are led finally to ask, "Why did this happen?" Only then will we pay attention to the theme and be ready for the lesson it has to teach us.

Essays may begin with a theme, but most narratives, except for allegories like *The Divine Comedy*, *Pilgrim's Progress*, and *Animal Farm*, are born from the impulse to tell a good story rather than push any philosophical dogma.

Even with the essay, there is usually an incident that prompts the writing: a car accident, the untimely death of a loved one, a new threat to the environment.

Once you've finished your first draft, examine the text for clues that relate to your chosen theme—subtle, yet revealing details. There should be objects or incidents in the story that stand for aspects of the theme. These symbols must work as organic elements of the story first, and symbols second.

Novels are not expected to be didactic, like tracts or morality plays; nevertheless, in varying degrees of implicitness, even the "purest" works of fictional art convey a philosophy of life. Ultimately, all good fiction is entertainment, and if it instructs or enlightens it does so best through enchanting the reader.
—Anthony Burgess

#84

GO WITH GOD, BUT WRITE WITH THE DEVIL

This is evil we're talking about, a cauldron of pain stirred by a pitchfork.

Writing not only records conflict, it begins and ends with, romanticizes, emphasizes, and takes its very life from conflict.

It can even be argued that the only reason to include love stories and comedy, pastoral splendor and puppy dogs in your work, is so that when you pull out a knife and stab your character through the skull and into his hot brain, it's that much more gruesome. Violence hits hardest on a calm stage.

What all this means for you as the creator of memorable mayhem is, unfortunately, a rich and miserable descent. How far you go into the horror of plain truth will be determined by your strength. You must be healthy, physically and psychologically, for this journey. Otherwise, you might drink too much, like Hemingway, Dylan Thomas, and F. Scott Fitzgerald, who all understood how dark life could be, and made it darker.

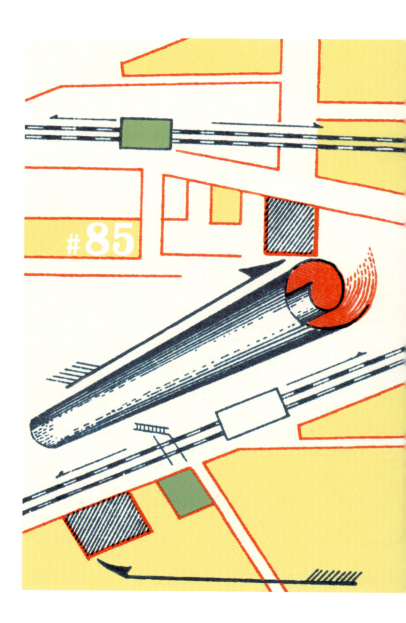

#85

RULE # 85

RESOLVE ALL
CONFLICTS BY THE END
OF THE STORY

A strong ending is most important because here you seal the package tight. The position demands of the author his utmost and ultimate brilliance. It is so foreboding and difficult that the anticipation of finally wrapping things up frightens us a little. There are countless writers out there with unfinished manuscripts, and this is one reason why.

It may not be a "happily ever after" ending, but something must be accomplished. Whatever was wrong has been made right, or about right. Rick loses the girl in *Casablanca* but walks off with nobility and the start of "a beautiful friendship." At the end of *Woman Warrior* the sound of the nomads' flutes rises into the night sky. In *The Great Gatsby* the green light at land's end still shines.

You can kill off your protagonist as long as hope lives on, and you get this with an image that represents the continuation of life.

86

RULE # 86

WRITING IS THE VEHICLE FOR **TRUTH**

Be honest.

The sheer power of a story, honestly presented, can transcend lapses in craft. Writers like James Michener, Henry James, and Ayn Rand enjoyed stellar careers because of the content of their work, not the beauty of their prose.

Story must be your motivator. Wanting to be a writer in the abstract will get you a drawer full of unpublished pages. Wanting to tell a story is something else. Think of yourself as a story-teller, and you'll cut through to real writing.

Where do honesty and truth come in? Ah. In the story.

Something happens. You get angry. "I have to tell this story to the world," you say. Maybe you write to make things right. You spin stories like charms to ward off bad luck. Stories born from hate and love, which are born from a genuine moment in time.

Why do writers write? Because it isn't there.
—Thomas Berger

87

MAINTAIN THE TRANCE OF VERISIMILITUDE

A way to remember the definition of verisimilitude is to think of art as "very similar" to real life.

All writers follow the strategy. They depict some kind of authentically appointed world and hope their creation brings us into it as participants. When this happens we suspend disbelief and enter a trance that makes us part of the story, unnoticed eavesdroppers.

The trance is delicate, like being under hypnosis, and the slightest interruption will cause it to shatter.

The best examples of breaking the trance come from movies, like a scene of cowboys riding the range in the Old West ... and there's a jet or a contrail in the sky; a person smoking a cigarette that gets longer in the next frame; a shot of people adrift in a life raft in mid-ocean, only there's a line of surf in the background; a village in medieval England with telephone poles.

The all-time prize for shattering verisimilitude has to go to Spielberg's use of the red coat in *Schindler's List*. Here's a black-and-white movie and we're into it as a brilliant period piece, and then here comes a little girl in a red coat. Everything around that coat, including the girl, is still black-and-white, but the coat is an important symbol, you see. The problem is that it screams, "I'm a device, a bit of digital artistry!" It says, "You're watching a movie!" when before that you were watching a life. Spielberg does this a lot, tosses in little bloops to remind us that the art is unreal. Dialogue offers another avenue for screwing up verisimilitude. Whatever time in history your characters work or live, they must speak accordingly, using appropriate phrases. Don't mix the idioms of popular contemporary culture in with scientists building the atomic bomb or warriors at the gates of Troy. Robert Oppenheimer would never say, "I can dig it," nor Achilles say, "Bring it on."

As wide-ranging as your imagination may be, whether you take flight into strange landscapes through science fiction, surrealism, or fantasy, ground your readers in their known universe.

For the most part, your vocabulary should be plain, sixth- to eighth-grade level. Your sentences short. Your scenes familiar. Help your readers come to feel at home in your prose.

Robert Frost addressed this notion when he said that "in literature it is our business to give people the thing that will make them say, 'Oh yes, I know what you mean.' It is never to tell them something they don't know, but something they know and hadn't thought of saying. It must be something they recognize."

Remember, your readers will demand artifice that doesn't seem artificial.

Art is a selective re-creation of reality according to an artist's metaphysical value-judgments.
—Ayn Rand, *The Romantic Manifesto*

#88

WRITING OFFERS
HOPE

You can write about blood and fire, human bodies scorched like forgotten cookies, about misery, torture, the lost infant with his throat slit, a family seed snuffed out, the extinction of a rare and elegant species (and we think in our atavistic arrogance that humans are the most rare and elegant on the planet), about shattered innocence, valiance unrewarded, betrayal by the people we loved most.

But in the end there must be a glimpse of gold, the first bright feather of a rare bird reborn from the ashes of a mythical bonfire.

One of the great traditions of art is that it provides hope. Beyond food and shelter, it's what keeps us alive. Especially today. For readers beset by the catastrophes of our modern world, hope is the most crucial sentiment. Make your audience gasp at suspenseful or wondrous adventures, but get them home safely. Let them breathe easy once more. Even if the memory of your astonishing story haunts them for years to come.

#89

RULE # 89

THINK ABOUT YOUR READERS

Writing is a double art. It takes two people to complete the process, and the demands upon the second party, the reader, are considerable. So make it easy.

Your audience represents the most highly trained in the world. Like writers, readers must use their imaginations, keep track of subplots and backstories, analyze the psychology of characters, make sense of conflicting philosophies, apply research to science, and become emotionally involved. Reading is an art in itself.

You must honor it with clarity.

If you want to answer the question, "Who is your audience?" look in the mirror. You're not only the primary reader, but those dear souls for whom you write are a lot like you. Same interests, background, similar passions.

Write something you'll all appreciate.

Write to be read.
—Ken Macrorie

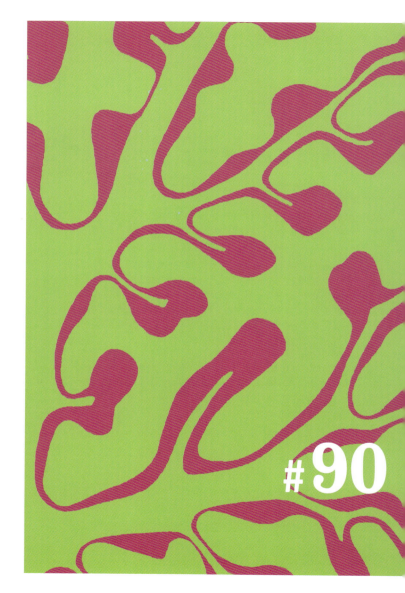

#90

RULE # 90

REVISE WITH A CRITICAL EYE AND OUTSIDE HELP

You can prevent your otherwise promising-to-the-point-of-perfection narrative from unraveling into stupidity by listening to the advice of your best critical reader. The one who stops you from embarrassing yourself before the work goes public.

Your trusted critical reader probably shouldn't be your spouse, best friend, or former teacher, but, if you're lucky, the smartest, harshest, least easy to impress person you know. Hand your manuscript over and then get out of the way. Let the reader read. Ask no questions. If too much time lapses, you've failed. Get the pages back. Find out how far the reader got, and ask for an assessment to that point. Then start revising. Remember, your work should be so gripping that your friend shifts priorities to read it, all of it.

By now you should have enough critical distance from the piece that you can see what's wrong.

And remember: The two greatest teachers are repetition and shame. Cut the offending material, change the rest accordingly, and resubmit.

91

ART SHOWS UP IN
REWRITING

Revise, revise.

You never get it on the first try. Never. Unless you're a natural like John Updike, whose prodigious volume of work would bury ten of his competitors, you'll need many drafts before reaching a polished and professional final.

Creating a manuscript is a lot like putting up a tree for Christmas. You first make a fresh cut on the trunk and mount it in a stand, then you position the tree in the room, fill the basin with water, and unpack your lights and decorations. That's your rough draft, the basic structural component upon which you hang the real beauties of your presentation.

Next you string the lights, which will enhance the dimension and depth of the tree, illuminating its outline and interior branches. Finally you arrange the glass globes, frosted angels, paper birds, and the varicolored baubles and bright icicles.

With each stage, you step back to evaluate how the project is coming along. You rearrange elements. Add there. Cut here. You want that perfect balance of shimmer and shine, of red and silver and green.

The tree has become a work of domestic art, like the book you're writing. In this final phase it eclipses itself and seems to be floating. You've noticed this before, in other fine works, that phenomenon of transcendence.

All because you kept revising until it was right.

I was working on the proof of one of my poems all the morning, and took out a comma. In the afternoon I put it back again.
—Oscar Wilde

GET DISTANCE FROM YOUR WORK

Often in the throes of creation, you might write something so fabulous it blinds you to how bad it really is. Maybe it has to do with the weird hours writers keep. You're too excited by this magnificent product and you send it out immediately. The world shouldn't have to wait for this! It could be the manuscript that lands you a spot on *The New York Times* best-seller list, a Pulitzer, a Nobel, a movie deal. Wow.

Whew. What a mistake.

The only one who should have to put up with the immediate reading of your material is your patient spouse. If you're not married, you've got no one. And there is no such thing as a patient spouse. You're the one who has to be patient.

In plain English: No one but you gets an immediate reading.

Put your work away when you're done, and let it sit. At least a week. Start another project in the meantime so your brain can shift away from the rhythms of the old text.

Then come back to it with icy objectivity.

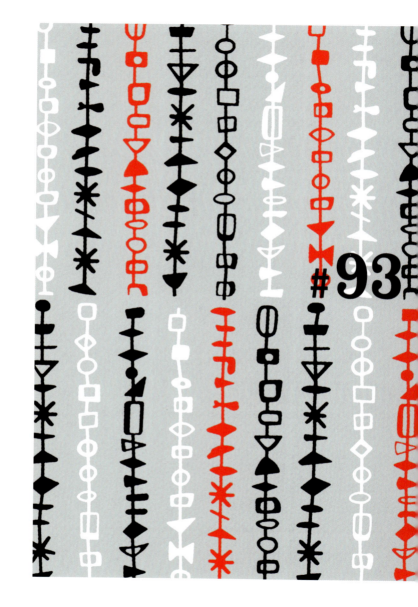

\#93

RULE # 93

REVISE FOR
SPEED

In the days before computers, a writer would literally have to cut and paste. That's what those commands on your PC refer to, kids, except that back then we used actual scissors and glue.

When we cut up a page and transferred the elements, an interesting thing happened: We learned to cut more than paste. And the resulting shorter copy read better.

An old formula says that the second draft should be 10 percent shorter than the first. The third draft 10 percent shorter than that. And the result equals what? A net reduction of 19 percent?

As you revise, try to cut your manuscript by at least 10 percent—that alone should improve the pacing. If you find that for every scene you trim, there's another you want to expand, ask yourself, "How does this further the plot?"

If it doesn't, let it go.

Show me where you looked up from the page, and I will cut, with the ink-sharp razor of cold, quick revision, the offending line.
—R. James Morris

TRUST THE MUSE OF REVISION

For the ancient Greeks there were nine muses, the goddesses of inspiration and the arts: Calliope, Clio, Erato, Euterpe, Melpomene, Polyhymnia, Terpsichore, Thalia, and Urania. But there should have been a tenth muse, the muse of revision. Call her Elora, which is Greek for light. Let her symbol be a lamp of midnight oil.

Revision is that important, and the whisperings of such a muse are every bit as sacred as those hallowed moments when fresh visions and ideas first come to you.

Keep your mind open to alternatives. And dedicate your heart to the process.

Faced with the assignment of finalizing a poetry manuscript for publication, William Butler Yeats said, "Months of rewriting. What happiness!" And he meant it.

Yeats knew. The procedure for fine art leads inexorably to editing, and all great writers have learned to be their own first, last, and most heartless editors.

When you sit down to create, forget about the rules. Just write the way you would tell the story to a friend.

Once that is done, review the pages in this book. The rules apply less to composition than they do to the glories of revision. They will help you shape a manuscript of professional quality.

Write before you read. Then rewrite after you read. Repeat.

What happiness.

#95

IF YOU CAN BE MISREAD, YOU WILL BE

Give your readers an opportunity to see or hear something you never intended and they'll jump at it, often in embarrassing ways. It happened in three popular songs, Jimi Hendrix's "Purple Haze," Peter, Paul, and Mary's "Puff the Magic Dragon," and Celine Dion's theme from the movie Titanic, "The Heart Goes On."

The chances for misinterpreting your writing usually come with an accidental double entendre. You record a scene of a man with his hand in his pocket and a smile on his face and you didn't mean it—but someone inevitably sees it—as risqué.

Control the intent of your content. Allowing for ambiguity will usually have readers focussing on the least favorable of options, when you want only the best.

Say all you have to say in the fewest possible words, or your reader will be sure to skip them; and in the plainest possible words or he will certainly misunderstand them.
—John Ruskin.

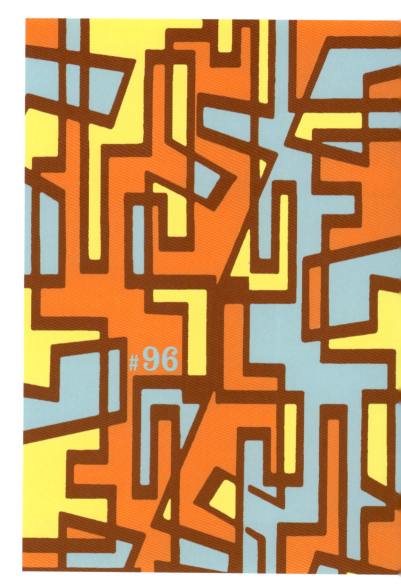

#96

ULTIMATELY, CONTENT MATTERS MORE THAN CRAFT

Witness the success of *The Notebook*, by Nicholas Sparks. This former *New York Times* No. 1 bestseller is so badly written, so poorly plotted, so rife with wooden characters that it's laughable.

Ah, but there's a catch here. How do you explain it's success?

The key is the book's irresistible frame: An old man in a nursing home goes to an upper floor every morning to visit another patient, a woman his age. He introduces himself to her each time because she has Alzheimer's and can't remember him. Then he sits down and reads to her from a notebook that he writes in during the night. The story he reads is their story—from the time they met and became young lovers until now. You see, this woman who can no longer remember his name or their history together is his wife.

That story of theirs is rendered in prose that would be considered mediocre in middle school, but never mind. The frame really touched readers' hearts. People still talk about it.

Do pay the utmost attention to your craft. Never let anyone accuse you of shoddy workmanship. But, above all, find a good story to tell.

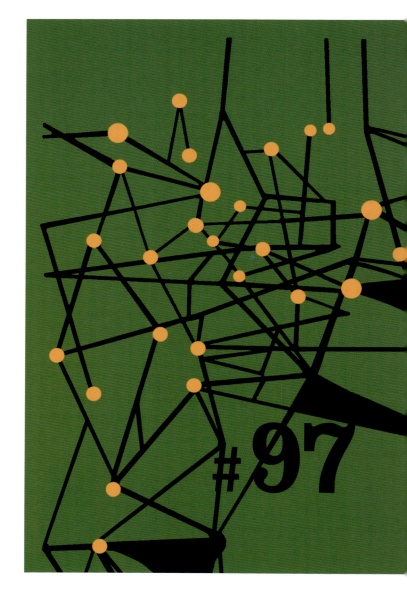

#97

RULE # 97

KNOW HOW TO SELL IT

What's the secret to getting an agent or publisher? Write a good book.

It takes more than this, however. You must sell the good book you've written, and this means mastering the "ten-second pitch." You've got ten seconds to impress editors. Great title? Fine. Got that. Now, what's the story about?

Editors (and later the book-buying public) want some idea of the plot before they begin reading your winning prose. In twenty-five words or less write down at least the general premise. Here are sample premises for two recent bestsellers:

> *A young boy in England discovers he is descended from wizards: The Harry Potter series.*

> *The murder of a curator in the Louvre sets off a search for the true Holy Grail: The DaVinci Code.*

After you've written a twenty-five-word teaser, it will be easier to write a one-page synopsis and then a ten- to fifteen-page synopsis. Books are often sold on these things alone: the title, twenty-five words, one-page synopsis, and writing sample.

STUDY THE
BOARD

As with chess and checkers, konane and Parcheesi, you're playing a game of calculated risk. More like solitaire at first, but then you face off against the competition.

Learn to win. You'll get close. Then further away. But if you keep at it, the strategies for victory will reveal themselves to you.

The metaphor relates to the market, and where you might fit in and make a name (a byline) for yourself. Really, you can publish anywhere you want, in *The New Yorker*, the *Los Angeles Times*, in scholarly or professional journals, with Simon & Schuster, Viking, Knopf. Name it. Wherever you want ... with two qualifications.

You must be fairly bright (and you are, or you wouldn't be reading this book), and you must commit to thoroughly researching your target publication. This means reading many, many copies and figuring out what the editors are looking for. In terms of both style and content. Then you pattern a submission that closely matches what you see in those pages. When you feel it's ready, send it off and get rejected.

Learn from the rejection, and try again. And again. It takes inestimable quantities of time, study, and patience. But the formula works.

The metaphor also applies to how you compose your work. First step: outline. Make a plan and stick to it. Build a framework, and then fill it in with words.

Study the game, ascertain your goal, make a plan, and see it through with patience and persistence, one move at a time.

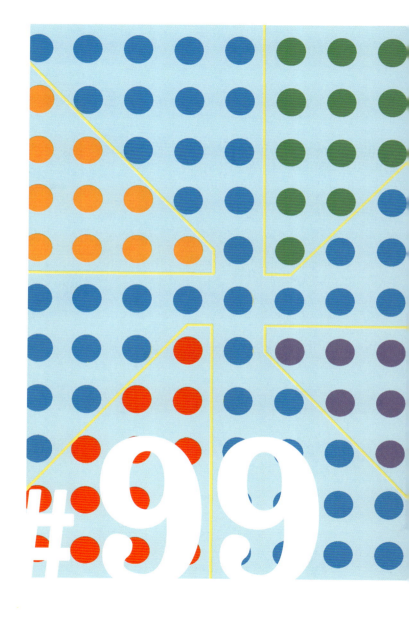

#99

99

SUBMIT A PROFESSIONAL
MANUSCRIPT

Those black marks on the white page have a certain appearance, a "terrain of the prose." On their own, in spite of whatever meaning we may give them as things representing thought, words are also graphic entities. Their arrangement on the page should be visually appealing.

Your manuscript should invite the reader in and constantly reward him for his time. Do this with white space, short paragraphs, sections of properly punctuated dialogue. As the eye travels over this graphic terrain it appreciates variety—an occasional parenthesis, a dash, a numeral.

Use white paper, conventional fonts with serifs (which have barbs to slow the reader and allow him to savor your words). Times and Palatino are preferred, 12 pica. Use an unjustified right margin on your submission pages. Provide neat, unwrinkled pages, 1.25-inch side margins, 1-inch top and bottom.

Proofread several times for mistakes, especially for spelling. We call it "spelling" because you do cast a magical spell with words, so make sure they're correct.

100

ASPIRE TO REACH A UNIVERSAL AUDIENCE

Shakespeare was smart. He knew to make a living as a writer he had to appeal to everyone, from paupers to aristocrats. So he staged for the people of London a series of terrific plays that ran the gamut from profound philosophy to sword fights, from taboo sex to farts.

The Globe Theater, where most of Shakespeare's plays appeared, gave the playwright a perfect audience, a cross section of society. For the "groundlings"—the poor people who paid a penny for admission to the theater courtyard, and stood or sat on the ground in front of the stage—Shakespeare provided "dumb shows and noise," the pageant of spectacle. For the more educated patrons—those who could afford seats in the Globe's boxes—he spun philosophy. His plays cut through class and station. There were depictions of war to entertain young men and soldiers; and romance for the lovers; the intrigues of court for the powerful; irascible children for parents; and poetry for each and all on a mild autumn day.

He remains popular to this day. Witness the recent Shakespeare films, community theater productions, and the rock-solid reputation of his work in English classes. It isn't just the intellectuals who appreciate his genius. Poet Robert Graves once said, "The remarkable thing about Shakespeare is that he really is very good, in spite of all the people who say he is very good."

So there you have it. All because Shakespeare wrote for everyone, from groundlings to kings.

Make for yourself such an audience. Write beyond just you and your friends. Challenge yourself. Aim higher. Aim lower. Target a more universal audience.

> *My books are water; those of great geniuses*
> *are wine—everybody drinks water.*
> —Mark Twain

EVALUATING YOUR OWN WORK

There should be big words in some of your sentences, but are they defined by context? If a reader doesn't have time to consult a dictionary, can he follow your thoughts anyway?

Do you balance philosophy with "dumb-show and noise"?

In your simplest stories, is there another level for the reflective reader to explore?

If you don't aspire to be a modern Shakespeare (but you should—come on, aspire to be the best!), are you at least trying to reach the same diversified audience he did? Give your work several different readings from varying points of view. Will your writing entertain everyone?

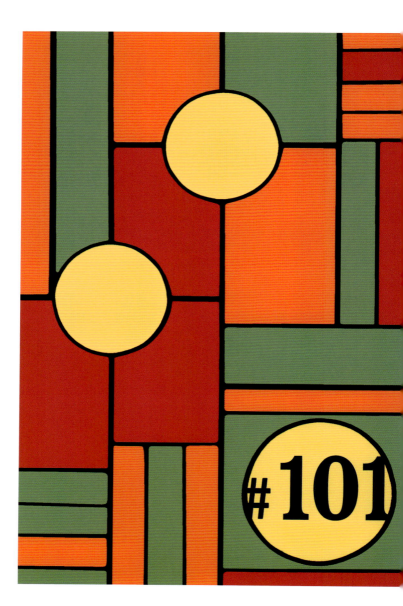

#101

EMBRACE THE WISDOM OF OPPOSING VIEWS

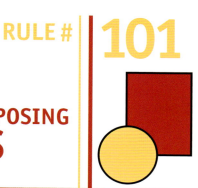

All these rules, pressed far enough, contradict each other. Such is the nature of rules for art.

Little wonder, then, that iconoclasts prosper. Icons mean nothing to the human heart, and their destruction is an iconographic gesture. The antitheses of life are inescapable.

It has been said that a real sign of intelligence is to be able to hold two or more contrasting ideas in your head at once. Things like "the beginning is the most important part," but "the punch line is at the end." "Trust your own voice" but "imitate others." "Think of writing as a hobby," but "be professional," but "be wild."

In the end, all that matters is your passion and the journey it takes you on. What seems important to you one day will be folly the next. But that's life. And that's writing.

Other people can tell you how to create scenes, structure plots, turn thought into poetry, and phrase into song. They will impart the lessons they have learned, and do it with such authority that you want to apprentice yourself to them, become an acolyte, a follower, a devotee, a sheep. For a while, what they tell you will help.

But if you're any good, you'll break away on your own—the way every serious writer must. You'll cancel out the rules, return to the nest of creativity that is your desk, sit tall in your chair, and let pure inspiration guide your pen. Just that, inspiration, those strange voices called fancy or "articulate dreams" or the whisperings of the muses, those voices that come in fragments until you write them down, listen again, and write some more. What you hear will expand and begin to make sense only through the singular expression of your art. Rules? Ha! All you need is a sensitive ear, a solid surface, a clean sheet of white bond, the unimpeded flow of ink, and the words of a world of your own making.

If they give you ruled paper, write the other way.
—Juan Ramón Jiménez

APPENDIX

EVALUATION GUIDE FOR YOUR WRITING
Questions to Ask About Your Work

1. How original is the title? Does it electrify you? Make you want to read this work?

2. Is the first sentence a "hook" that pulls your eye into the text? Are there visual images in the first sentence? Can you see this fictional world? If the opening scene is not exciting (as it should be), does the quality of writing sustain you? Is there poetry in the language?

3. By the end of the first paragraph, do you sense conflict? Whose problem is it? Is it internal conflict or external?

4. Do the opening paragraph and first scene follow the standard graph in terms of ascending action and climax? As the story continues, does this pattern repeat, with each scene more compelling than the last?

5. Where are you? Is the setting detailed and evocative? Is it crucial to the story? How authentically are rooms furnished? How is the weather? Do the characters follow the "terrain" of the setting up or down? In other words, as you ascend along the standard plot graph, are you going uphill in this fictional world? And, when you go higher, do you encounter more difficulties? You should be, or what's the sense in climbing?

6. Who are the characters? Are they eccentric enough to be interesting without crossing into caricature? Who is the

protagonist? What lesson does the protagonist seem to need? How do the other characters help teach this lesson? Who is the villain? How do the villain and protagonist play off (and symbolically balance) each other? Will most readers identify with the protagonist and vicariously participate in the learning process?

7. Does the dialogue sound like real people talking? Is there enough sarcasm or anger or frustration (conflict/angst) in the dialogue? Are the values of the characters brought out in what they say?

8. Is there more exposition than there should be? Are you telling or showing? Remember, you're in show business.

9. Does the protagonist have an epiphany (the moment of realization) just before or just after the climax? What does the protagonist realize?

10. Is the climax a (metaphorical or actual) fiery explosion? How do the actions and personality of the protagonist trigger the climax? And what is the lesson?

11. Are the protagonist's accomplishments recognized in the denouement? Is there an awards ceremony? Does the denouement have a climax?

12. What is the theme? Is there a moral? How do objects in the story symbolize the struggle of the protagonist? Even if the story doesn't end on a happy note (although most should—there are enough sad endings in the real world), will the readers feel edified and educated? Have they spent their time wisely with this work of art?